Barrio Writers™

Empowering Teens Through Creative Writing...

NINTH EDITION

A collection of works by teens for teens, teachers, & our communities

STEPHEN F. AUSTIN STATE UNIVERSITY PRESS
2018

Logo Design: Jimmy Prieto

For more information Contact:

STEPHEN F. AUSTIN STATE UNIVERSITY PRESS
414 Aikman Drive, LAN 203
P.O. BOX 13007
NACOGDOCHES, TEXAS 75962
sfapress@sfasu.edu
sfasu.edu/sfapress
936-468-1078

ISBN: 978-1-62288-215-1

Contents

Victoria Garcia / 11

Klarissa Ugalde / 14

Brianna Arriaga / 17

Madyson Claeys / 20

Abeni Brown / 22

Blanca Serrano / 25

Xcaret Meneses / 26

Breanna Lee / 29

Kimberly Phou / 33

Briann Marie Allen / 35

K.J. Huey / 37

Grecia Peñaloza / 40

Clarissa Camacho / 42

Kaiss Robles / 44

AVK / 48

Nathaniel Lopez / 52

Isabel Garza / 54

Adriana Galvan / 57

Meagan McQuein / 58

Jose Salvador Chavez Chavez / 63

Shaelyn Westbrok / 65

Aphra Ezar / 67

Stuart Olson Beal / 76

Alma Sarahi Tlachi / 79

Nomar Santana / 80

Adrian Michael Graham / 82

Elizabeth Whitmire / 84

Olivia Goodley / 85

Jasmine C. Bell / 87

Alexis Williams / 89
Noble Peck / 91
Gracie O'Dell / 92
Isis Rivera / 94
Minh Ly / 96
Robert Andaluz / 97
Adrian Gutierrez / 98
Pedro Flores / 99
Logun Claeys / 101
Courtney Michelle Roberts / 102
Cesar Villanueva / 103
Alexis Avila / 104
Ricardo Morales Perez / 106
Taylor Gates / 109
David Kotkin / 110
Anonymous / 111
Taylor Nicole Williams / 112
Samantha Sanchez / 113
Jose Vega / 121
Tony Robertson / 127
Evelyn Bahena Casas / 128
Sophie Johnson / 130
Kasia Driver / 133
Tytrice Conor / 135
Jorge Molina / 136
Eduardo Jose Gutierrez / 137
Ashley Beltran / 138
Lindsey Thompson / 139
Ari Scroggins / 143
Za Khia KeIzhane' Davis / 147
Brandon Spigner / 149
Gabriela Garcia / 150

Eliana Rodriguez / 153
Crystal Hernández / 155
Julio Diaz / 157
Adrian / 164
Gisselle Lizama / 166
MJ Watson / 167
Fernando Reyes / 170
Zion Angelo Williams Flores / 174
Alexis Martinez / 176
Cesar Lopez / 178
Alyssa Becnel / 179
Amy Arelly O. / 181
Stephanie Gomez / 183
Christian Sida / 185
Hannah M. Abbott / 188
Cameron Daniels / 190
Cristian Dominguez / 192
Patricia Limon / 195
Giselle Godinez / 197
Adrian Martinez / 202
Jackie Ramirez / 203
Rafael Flores / 205
Julia Gomez-Rangel / 208
Cassidy Lapierre / 210
Esmeralda Zenaida Rivera / 212
Rosalinda Avitia Segura / 214
Moe / 220
Alma Peguero / 223
Shyla Driver / 227
Yasmeen Davila / 230
Keona D. Redmon / 233

Writing Advisor's Note

I sat with Ricardo in front of a computer. His strong hands pecked keys on the keyboard slowly one by one. Ricardo was about sixteen, a cheerful friendly Latino kid who was happily willing to be friends with anyone and everyone. He had attended the Barrio Writers week that my colleagues and I organized. It was Friday. We had over twenty students in the computer lab rapidly typing their final submissions for us to send to Sarah Rafael Garcia to be published in the 8th edition of the Barrio Writers anthology. I kept my eye on Ricardo. Since his creative writing piece was rather long, I knew it would take him a while to get it typed into the computer. I quietly asked him, "Ricardo, you doing ok?" He smiled and answered softly, "Yes ma'am." An hour later, Ricardo was the only one left in the computer lab. I had been busily helping other students. I walked back to check on his progress... He still had quite a long section of writing yet to type. I was concerned he would miss out on some of the other Barrio Writers workshop activities for the day so I asked him, "Ricardo, would you mind if I typed some of that for you?" His face immediately washed with relief, and he slid over to the next seat. "Yes ma'am," he said.

I told him I thought his piece was amazing, and I loved his perspective. Then he began to tell me his story. He said that when he was a toddler, he was diagnosed with a type of progressive glaucoma that would leave him blind if untreated. His family lived in Mexico, and the medical care he needed was only available in the United States. His mother and father chose to make the dangerous border crossing and travel far away from everything they had ever known. In his parents' minds, they did not have a choice. Their son's eye sight was worth the danger, the journey, the money and the move. Ricardo said that once they arrived in the United States, he was able to get the medical treatment to save some of his vision. He told me that if they had not made that choice, he would have been completely blind. Ricardo was grateful for his parent's choice. In the U.S. his parents found work in the chicken farms. His family lived in a small, one-room cinder blocks house. Ricardo said there was often no heating and air conditioning, and his family often shared the space with other workers and their families. They had to be ready at any time to go into the chicken farm building and work. The whole family would help because the physical labor was difficult and time consuming. He shared that his mother was sensitive to the poor air quality and heat in the chicken barn and sometimes would pass out during the work. Ricardo mentioned that working in the chicken barn is one of his earliest memories of the United States. He then went on to tell me how much it hurt him to hear the President talk of walls and deporting immigrants. He stated, "my family and I are so grateful to the people of the United States for my sight, and we work hard to make a living. We do jobs that no one else wants. I just don't understand why some people hate us."

I sat in the chair stunned. I was honored and moved that he told me his story, and at the same time horrified at what his family had endured with such a grateful attitude. I said, "Ricardo, thank you for sharing that with me. I cannot wait to see what you can accomplish with your life." He smiled and said, "I'm going to go to the other room now." And I said, "sounds good, see you in a few minutes." I just sat there. I couldn't continue typing his piece. I was not worthy of his words.

The importance of Barrio Writers weighed in my heart and mind. Barrio Writers is designed to empower, to inspire, to help youth learn to use their voice as an agent of change in our society. Paradoxically, I found myself the one inspired, empowered, and passionate to help change society for Barrio Writers like Ricardo. Instead of me inspiring him, he had inspired me. Instead of me educating him, he had educated me. As a middle-aged, white woman with a PhD in education, the epitome of white privilege, this youth had completely turned my white arrogance upside down, and I will never be the same.

Barrio Writers workshops give youth like Ricardo a place to upset the systemic balances of power in our society and share the importance of their story. The Barrio Writers workshop allowed Ricardo a voice and a platform to share his amazing perspectives, stories, and experiences. This one-week, summer writing workshop provides a space for diverse kids in the community to hold power over their own story, and share it in their own words; to connect and influence other kids and adults; to potentially make our society a better and more accepting place for all beginning with their small circles; and to educate ignorant well-schooled people like myself on the important connection between voting, policy, and people that often gets swept into the cracks within the current public school system.

Youth like Ricardo, with powerful and influential character, experiences, and stories, will be the next generation of change-makers in the United States. Many times, schools and society cannot or will not allow the type of writing you will read in the holy pages that follow. Read with courage, compassion, empathy, and be mindful of how you can allow the youth the space and opportunity to tell their story.

To Ricardo and every other brave Barrio Writer, you have changed my life. All your stories, your experiences, your cultures, your religions, your races, your ethnicities, your sexual orientations, and your gender make you who you are. Please tell us your story. You are important, you are valued, and we as a nation need to hear your voice.

—Dr. Chrissy J. Cross
Assistant Professor,
Stephen F. Austin State University
Barrio Writers Writing Advisor,
Nacagdoches, Texas

Preface

Barrio Writers (BW) is a creative writing program founded by author Sarah Rafael García, which provides free college level writing workshops to teenagers in underserved communities. In the summer of 2009, thirty students came together to form the first Barrio Writers chapter in Santa Ana, California, a non-profit reading and writing program that aims to empower teens through creative writing, higher education, and cultural arts.

BW is a non-profit program that offers workshops and additional one-on-one tutor hours for one week throughout the academic summer break. Students receive college-level workshops to build skills in reading, grammar, creative writing, critical-thinking and freedom of expression through cultural arts. The session includes guest writers who serve as role models in our neighborhoods and support youth aspirations.

The BW program thrives through its community collaboration. By aligning with universities and Resistencia Bookstore, BW participants are exposed to diverse activities provided in the surrounding areas while in turn, give support to the local cultural arts and community resources. Most recently, we have partnered with the Nicholas Academic Center in Santa Ana and the Yolo County Library in Davis in California, along with the Center of Studies of the Southwest at Texas State University in San Marcos, Texas. All three chapters united to form a new community of BW along with our long-standing chapter in Santa Ana, California, which was hosted by CSUF Grand Central Art Center, and our additional chapters: University of Texas at Austin, University of Houston and Stephen F. Austin State University in Nacogdoches, Texas A&M Corpus Christi, and Universtiy of Texas at El Paso.

The program strives to present alternative forms of expressions through cultural art collaboration in the community. The summer workshops culminate with a live reading, which allows BW to present final pieces to our community and reach a wider audience by potential media coverage and book sales. The written works submitted by teens from the multiple chapters are published in an anthology collection. It is our goal to include all chapters in each annual edition to form a diverse youth community beyond the workshops.

BW participants are between the ages of thirteen to nineteen years old and reside in the surrounding area of the local chapters. By opening workshops to all levels of students from local schools and neighborhoods, BW includes teenagers from diverse circumstances to participate and share their lives with our society. We also encourage for college and university students up to the age of 21 to participate as peers obtaining higher education.

One goal of the program is to publish an anthology of written works demonstrating the diverse backgrounds of teenagers that can be used in and out of the classroom. Barrio Writers is a collection of works by teens for teens, teachers and our communities. All profits from the book are returned to the

BW program for future years. The long-term goal is to publish a new edition each year with hopes that more neighborhoods will adopt the program and more teachers will use the BW book in the classroom. The BW program and its annual anthology are designed to empower the teenage community while establishing a self-sufficient educational program that will represent community pride, perseverance, and endless possibilities for following generations.

Victoria Garcia

Though I don't know my story yet, I know I am meant to create one. I am currently eighteen years old. I was born on February 26, 1999 in Houston, Texas. Although the highest grade I earned in any English class I have taken was a high B average, writing has become one of my more favored hobbies. Ever since the second grade, when my class was assigned to write poems to present in front of everyone, I became interested in writing. From poems to mindless drabbles, the older I became the more I wrote. To me, writing is a way to expand and connect; you can create different worlds or just reveal your own. It was not until just recently I realized what I wanted to do for a living. I will be attending university soon in hopes of graduating with a major in English and a Professional Writing concentration. I wish to be an author or even an editor. I also hope to someday connect and inspire people with my writing.

Mr. President

Mr. President, may I speak?
Can you give me that decency?
'Cause I've seen how you've treated my people
I've heard what you think about people like me
You say you want America great again
I can't think of a time in the books it was
'Cause I'm one quarter Native American
And three Hispanic
So this land was mine before Columbus thought to sail it
Yet there you stand behind a podium
Saying "send them back, the rapists and the terrorists"
But you seem to forget white is the original illegal immigrant
And you say we're pretty great
But this country was built on genocide and slavery
You say we're moving forward
If that's so why does it feel we're back in time
Before Civil Rights
Before Dr. King
And before "Muslim Ban" could even be a serious thing
You're single handily supporting racism
Even though I'm sure if we walked in
A person of color is hired to clean your expensive estates
And you'd be paying much below minimum wage
You say they're stealing jobs
But guess who is hiring them

This country isn't by the people, for the people
It's by the wealthy, for the white
And I'm tired of seeing people like I
Called names and shoved into fights
I'm tired of seeing people of different religion
Told "no, you can't come in"
Because their god isn't that of the favored "majority"
That why we're known only as "minorities"
But we're people
Breathing, living, and desperately trying
to get our voices over the white noise

Mr. President, please sit down, quit squirming in your seat
I know it's hard for you to hear from a woman like me
Especially when I say you're ruining my country
The one my ancestors lived on
Raised families on

Let me back track, you're not ruining it
Not completely
You're revealing and igniting it
Racism has always been there like serpents
on darkened streets
But we avoided it by closing windows and saying prayers
Now they're out of their cages
Causing more chaos than the people you seem to fear
And you forgive them
Only cause they're just like you

Mr. President, my people belong here
Just as much as you think you do

At the Dining Table

Sundays after church,
My Grandma let us eat on the patio
If it was hot, we had watermelon
Always red, always sweet
She'd take out the black seeds, point to our tummies and say
"Here is where the watermelon grows when you swallow those"
An oddly funny fear for every seed we accidentally ate

On cold days we sat at the dining table
Meant for eight, but only harbored us four kids
Sometimes my Grandma would join
Laugh and swap stories
Like the friend you always wanted

On holidays, the dining room was always full
People talking, playing, and arguing
No room for children, but even then, Grandma found us kids
Just to talk, mostly to listen
Like the ocean

Birthdays happened in the dining room too
We all aged with the wood
We all grew tired and weary
The kids no longer kids
But we still showed every year

At the dining table we stayed
Cause Grandma was sick one day
Late night or early early morning
If that's what you consider it

We got the news.

Grandpa sold the house
Everything was cleaned out
And from the dining table I watched
As memories moved away.

Writing Activity

1. Victoria Garcia chose to address her poem to 'Mr. President' as a "Native American" and "Hispanic." Does that make her letter/poem more powerful? Why? Write a poem to a politician that you think doesn't represent America well. Let them know what you think and why they're wrong. You don't have to send it to them.

2. Victoria's poem "At the Dining Table" is about home and how it can disappear in an instant. Write a poem about a time when something was taken away from you. What was it? What did it mean to you? Why is it gone?

Klarissa Ugalde

Klarissa is a 15-year-old girl who lives in San Marcos, Texas. She is a hard-headed person that speaks her mind. One of her hobbies, if you hadn't noticed, is writing. Klarissa writes with many purposes and joy.

The Sights of Memory

I feel history of the ones before, the faces of the people.
Just pictures seen that have so much more of a story.

The colors,
the patterns
appealing to my eyes
I wonder what they mean.
My mind leads me to question all of it, to try and see the true beauty and meaning of it all.
One stands out and makes memories come back to my mind.
Memories of sitting outside
with the sun glistening away
and the laughter through it all.

I hear silence but hear noise from all the sights.
The rapid sound of starting
a new page of writing.
The scratching of words
being crossed out.

They shout out to me and tell me to see, see what they mean.
I feel warmth, I feel peace from the joy of writing.
I feel at home, not from the room,
but from the pen moving silently on the paper.

Then, I hear the thought…….

Writing is peace.

A Better Life

I wish for her to stay. If she is taken, what will my life be?
My father is gone now, it is just us three.
School is my brother and I's safety. An education, she repeats, that's all she wants for us.
Where is my mother's safety?

I have learned how to read.
A further education is what we need.

Encouragement to succeed is what we are given.
She forces a smile, all the while missing the words our father would say,
still wishing she could have helped him stay.

The words my father mouthed as I'd seen him being told to come out from hiding.
"Make me proud, I love you."
I will do exactly what my father has told me to.

Why don't they see a better life is near?
Can't they see it's better here?

If she is taken, danger is what we'll see.
My mother needs to watch us grow.
If she is taken, I will not have a smile on the stage.
My heart will be filled with raged.

She shouldn't have to leave because of race,
or the pace of her spoken thoughts.
But they don't want us to speak up,
so silent we remain.

I want to stay here with my family,
and the only place known as home.

Dear Future Me

Dear Future Me,

We are fifteen years old right now. We are confused about what we are surrounded by. Heartless people of this world almost convince you what they say is true. They say no one has done it before. Dreams have obstacles. Obstacles we can overcome. Obstacles we will overcome. I wish our dreams are reached. I wish for us to learn beyond our comprehension. By now I hope you are reading this and saying Yes! Yes! Yes! I hope you finally found yourself in this wondrous world. I hope that we will know what we want to do for the rest of our life.

We will reach our goals.
We will be found.

--Past You

Writing Activity

1. Imagine a place you are familiar with and use your five senses to describe it.

2. At the beginning of the week, give the writers the free writing prompt called "Dear Past Me." This prompt works as a letter to your past self. Good questions to have the writers ask themselves is, "Is there something you wish you knew then that you can reflect on now? If you don't feel so different from your past self, how would you describe your development as a person?" This prompt helps the writers begin to evaluate their personal experiences, which is a great place for new and mature writers to start in the workshop.

3. Brainstorming: Try to think about someone who has a life story which sticks out in your mind. (Remember it doesn't have to be a person—your persona poem can be about a person, place, or thing) Your poem could be the persona of a fictional or nonfictional character. It could be about something or someone which exists in a book you read or has had their name appeared in a news article. What is their name, gender, occupation, sexual orientation, their story, etc.? Once you've chosen someone or something, give yourself the permission to imagine their thoughts. Imagine being them. As you begin writing, use "I," the first-person pronoun, to enter into the persona of this person, place, or thing. Where would they go? What would they want to tell you?

Brianna Arriaga

Her name is Brianna Arriaga. Fourteen is her age and making a difference is her goal. She is from Austin, Texas. Yet, she has been raised ALL around Texas. Her feet never still, her mind always running, and her words always inspiring. She's an athletic girl who broke records and made new ones. Her family is always by her side. Let not her size or physical appearance fool you. Cause her words will kick your ass. Giving goosebumps, inspiring words, and giving bad ass imagery. Showing you that the youth has something to say. To listen to them. Knowing that even the YOUTH has to go through stuff like you. She hopes her writing will make a difference and stand up to any and all communities. Barrio Writers is the first step. The next is making a difference.

Self Portrait

These lips. These lips tasted the bitter sweet taste of abuelas tamales. These lips have released words that said 'Fuck you' to people who put shame on me. These lips have kissed cheeks and foreheads to show that I care. Kissed lips to show I love you. Her lips, his lips. Does it really matter?

These cheeks which felt the pinch of tias love. These cheeks which have drowned in tears at night. These cheeks which have felt the force of anger and frustration.

This nose which smelt the sweet food from the kitchen. This nose has smelt the rain before it came, the grass in which it has been cut. This nose which smelt death once before.

These ears which has heard many things. My mother's voice, my father's commands. The music which slowly drifted me away. The crying and pain of others. Ugly words that came from others mouth. Words that don't come from mine. Words like…like…words that my fingers can't type.

These eyes…dear god…these eyes which saw MANY things. Love, hate, separation, A WALKING CHEETO PUFF! These eyes have poured out tears and saw many. These eyes has saw people being torn people be torn from their families. Babies being stripped from their mothers. Being placed in handcuffs and muffled sounds being heard. Different colored people going different ways. These eyes has seen only white people in history books. Flip the page and another one. Maybe one black person, yet they are in shackles. These eyes has seen so much shit. I am 14.yet what I've been through can only define my age.

So stop letting my ears hear ugly words. Let my nose stop smelling death. Let rain be the only thing that falls on my cheeks. Let my lips be free of what I can say instead of putting a finger to it. Let my eyes see something other than hate. Let my ears stop hearing the bullshit people tell me to help me sleep at night.

We, us kids

We don't like the labels you give us.
We don't take the bullshit you tell us.
We have answers to your questions. Your questions are: which part of Mexico are you from? How do you speak English so well? How many years have you been in the US?

Our answers are: we come from a part of Mexico where we never even stepped in. A part where our ancestors crossed from. We speak English so well because our parents taught us. Mama..papa..tia if we got a prize. I've been in the US since I was born. Since my mom PUSHED me out of her to give me a better life she had.

We, us kids that take the labels of illegal, don't know why you give it to us. Cause no one is illegal in this world. Aliens to your home. Trying to 'corrupt' your mind. Coming to your homeland, which was once ours.

We are the ones who take shit from people who take a look at us and then whisper lies which sting our ears and bind our minds. The only boarders that stop us are stop signs, our parent's words, and a period.

We don't like the labels you give us.
We don't take the bullshit you tell us.

We, us kids who get picked on, kicked out, pushed away because the color of our skin, are TIRED of it! We kids are aren't 'illegal'. We kids who don't have scars on our hands and feet like our grandparents. We kids who are scared to go come home and see our parents gone and knowing we ARENT next. We kids who were born on the 'land of the free, home of the brave.'

Generations to come

My voice is a voice of generations. More dangerous than a tantrum of a young infant. The deadliest of weapons. Shoot through the governments bulletproof ears. An arrow that can shoot over and over through the crucial of hearts. My words will knock you out and all you will see is darkness. Blackness…blackness that will fill the void and thoughts you will have. My words will make you think then rethink. My words will give you goosebumps throughout your arms. First a whisper then a loud scream. For when I am done, you will blankly stare at me. My words going over and over in your head. So when you hear a voice from a kid, look into their eyes. See the story hidden in them. Now tell me what do you see? Tell me what story they tell or what secrets are buried. Do you see the rivers they swam across? The fist they saw before THEY saw darkness? Their mothers face, telling them it's gonna be okay? Do you see the liquid that covers the road? Do you see my peoples blood fill the cracks on the street? The news will say they will always remember, yet a week later their focus is an invention for the future. That's if we have a future. ADULTS say we are a messed-up generation. Well who made this generation?

Now look into my eyes. What story do you see? Is it giving you goosebumps or should I keep talking?

Writing Activity

1. Have you ever seen a painter's self-portrait (think Frida Kahlo's many paintings)? Write a self-portrait in which you describe yourself as you are, how others see you, or how you want to be (not just your physical self but your inner self).

2. In "We, us kids," Brianna uses the communal "we" to express how her generation feels about the labels and stereotypes that adults project onto youth. Is there a person or group that you feel stereotypes a group or identity that you are a part of? If you could speak for that group, what would you say?

3. Brianna describes her words and their power by using sensory details. Write your own piece in which you compare something abstract like words or feelings to something visual or physical. How does this give them power?

Madyson Claeys

Her pen name is MC kitty, aka Mady, aka Madyson. She lives in Corpus Christi, Texas. She loves her family, even her brothers, and mom and dad. She loves music, writing, and tennis. She loves to read random books, not counting history books. She loves animals, especially monkeys and dolphins. She also likes kitties but prefers monkeys.

Goodbye My Friends

All those hurtful things you've done to me
You brought to me

Made all the voices tell me
Who I should be
Who I need to be

I need to be quiet
I need to sit alone
I can't trust anybody
I can't love myself
I'm worthless
I'm nothing
I can only stick to myself

HA!
Those are my monsters talking

The voices tell me my only friends are the monsters that are inside my head

That's all the enemies talking
Setting the rules

Well, I'm sorry my friend that's not who I am

I'm sorry my friend that's not what I want to hear

I'm sorry my friend I can't walk with you anymore

I can't run away with you anymore my friend
My monsters
I will never let you control me again

I won't let you
They may have hurt me
But I am strong
I am a fighter

I am me
And you are you
Goodbye my friend

The Fight Starts When the Crow Screeches

She stands on a land of eerie trees
The wind blowing through her hair
The crow cawing landing on her shoulder
Telling her to be ready they're almost here
She looks at the crow and nods giving the crow a pat on the head
Then looked up
The crow took flight into the sky of dark clouds
She looked straight ahead
Through the fog she sees shadow figures
Big and small
Short and tall
The crow screeches
She's ready
One more screech the crow makes
and the fight begins

Writing Activity

1. It's always interesting to find out what animals writers identify with. For Mady, she has always been interested in crows. Think of an animal you personally identify with, and write a fictional piece or a poem about the animal. You don't have to personify (give it human characteristics), but you should use the surroundings and natural habitat of the animal.

Abeni Brown

Abeni Jujianne Brown was born on July 21, 2003 in El Paso, Texas. Abeni has a wonderful family who sacrificed so much for her. Abeni's mother and father were both born and raised in Jamaica. They then traveled to the U.S., had her older brother Ajani, and then herself in El Paso, Texas. They officially found jobs and settled in Nacogdoches, Texas.

Abeni enjoys writing short stories, spoken word, and poems. In her free time, she enjoys playing the piano, violin and dancing to her favorite songs. She also loves her Jamaican cultural background and how it has influenced her as an individual today.

Abeni has enjoyed every second of Barrio Writers. She loves how she was able to better and expand her writing styles. Barrio Writers has increased her confidence and gave her a voice through her writing.

Little Black Girl

"You talk white."

"You act white."

"You are like a white girl in a black girl's body!"

These phrases are not made up. These confusing words are all put into an even more confusing sentence that kept me up for nights wondering what these people even meant. These sentences were said by both races white and black. These phrases clogged up her mind. These sentences were said by both races white and black.

The little black girl's mind was never the same when she stepped into class on her first day of middle school with high hopes and dreams. She opened her mouth at every question and made sure to pronounce every syllable correctly. It was lunch time and she would never forget the year, class period, and moment when a boy of her own race asked her with much disgust, "Do you want to be white?" The little black girl with cornrows at the time stared lifelessly at the boy of her own race and didn't say a word.

When the little black girl got home she stared at herself in the mirror and cried. She focused on her neatly cornrowed hair and wondered did she really want to be white?

The Last Namuh

Once upon a time on a planet called Htrae every second a Namuh is born but these Namuh beings are exquisitely special. They are born without a race to be stereotyped, an ethnicity to be distinguished by or a gender to be classified above or below. They are born without all the things they never had the possibility of changing

Although, these Namuh beings couldn't be any more different character wise, but they are all still one. How did the differentiate one from another? you might ask. The way they valued each other was through their mind, heart, and soul. Which is why a Namuh beings love and friendship for each other was unbreakable. They Namuh beings never based anyone at all on looks after all they didn't need a society when they had unity.

Where is Htrae located? you might ask too. It is located in the exact opposite direction of planet Earth.

One horrifying, dark, shady day which changed Htrae forever started when a human being from planet Earth looked through a telescope at planet Htrae. The human which was of a certain race decided to claim planet Htrae for themselves and hoped to find glorious gold there. But little did he know the treasure was the unbreakable love to Namuh beings had for each other. He gathered up his crew allowing only of his race and started his exploration to claim the land too good to be true that definitely wasn't of his own.

The human with the crew of the same race could not possibly travel in their spaceships without supplies. They studied rare magical books about the Namuh beings. They knew they had to somehow get rid of them. The humans were extremely biased. They didn't know how they could possibly communicate to the different beings without knowing their race, ethnicity, or gender.

What supplies did they bring? You might ask. They brought their worst disease called hatred equipped with pistols. They also brought along skin dyes to classify the Namuh beings race, pink and blue bracelets which they thought distinguished the Namuh's gender.

The Namuh beings were both joyful and fearful to have new company land on their ground. The human beings listened cautiously and suspiciously to their warm welcome. The humans thought the Namuh beings were savages that needed to be humanized.

The human told his crew of the same race to get the skin dyes, bracelets and pistols ready. The human beings pointed the pistols at the Namuhs who had a confused, hurt, and innocent look in their eyes. They threw up their hands and surrendered.

The human ordered the human beings to take several groups of Namuh's, adults and children, and dye their skin white, black, brown, red and yellow. The human also ordered the other human beings to place pink bracelets on one half of the Namuh beings and mark them as women. Then the human demanded the humans place blue bracelets on the other half of the Namuh's and classified them as men.

The human ordered the black Namuh's be killed, the brown Namuh's be sent to hard labor, the red and yellow Namuh's as servants and lastly the white Namuh's be sent back to Earth to learn the awful human ways.

The last Namuh that was not killed, or sent away, nor transformed into a human stood standing but little did the Namuh know that they had company. The human saw the Numah was staring lifelessly at the treasure he didn't understand why the human so much desired.

The Namuh heard the piercing growl of the human. The human's eyes turned the color of crimson blood. He gripped the pistol in his massive, veiny hands and pointed it toward the Namuh's chest where the Namuh's heart was a target.

"Boom!" The Namuh dropped dead. "That ought to teach you to stay away from my treasure," The human mumbled as he untied the treasure key from the Namuh's bloody neck.

The human walked proudly to the treasure chest and unlocked it. The human almost fainted to see the raw, veiny, still beating heart. The petrified human slowly turned to see the Namuh's chest had a huge hole larger than the bullet wound.

The human almost crying now turned his head slowly back around and noticed the heart wasn't even wounded but he noticed writing on the heart it spelled out.

UNBREAKABLE.

Epilogue

This concludes the tale of how a human's hurtful cold-blooded heart can change lives like never before.

Like today we relived in the past this tale. We were the first one to take others' land in the past as if it was our own.

When immigrants different from us come to "our" land which we stole, killed, and ripped native American families apart for. We must really think and ask ourselves who really were the original immigrants. Most often these people just like us came to support their families but as a country we drive them away.

We must stop this before we relive this tale in the future.

Writing Activity

1. In "Little Black Girl," Abeni writes about how it feels to have a part of your identity questioned or doubted. Have you ever had this kind of experience, where someone looks at you or hears something you say and wonders who you really are? Try writing a poem or essay about that experience.

2. What is the lesson behind "The Last Namuh?" Can you think of connections to current events taking place around the world or in your community? Think about writing an essay or a spoken word piece about a current event that affects you or a friend or family member in some way.

Blanca Serrano

Blanca was born in Cuernavaca, Morelos. She currently lives with her mother and attends church with her father. She is a student at the Nicholas Academic Centers and at Valley High School. She enjoys spending time with her pets and Best Friend Jackie. In the future, she wants to pursue a double major in East Asian studies and linguistics due to her love of Korean Culture.

I'm Sorry

Forgive me for clinging onto you
I long to show my remorseful face
Release me and you will cultivate curses
All this freedom created a toxic relationship
Being aware was not enough to hold me back
My lips are full of regrets
For all the damage I did I am sorry.

Writing Activity

1. Blanca plays with formatting and layout in her poem "Lost & Gained." Why do you think Blanca does this? Consider playing with the formatting of one of your poems.

2. The poem "I'm Sorry" is in the form of an apology. Try writing a similar poem. What are you sorry for? Why? Is this liberating? What do you feel in writing an 'apology?'

Xcaret Meneses

Born in Santa Ana, California on June 2002, Xcaret Meneses was raised, alongside an older sister, by two hardworking parents. Throughout her childhood, Xcaret's mother was constantly moving while her father had taken residency in a shabby, two-room apartment. Due to her mother, Xcaret has attended eight different schools and, to this day, is transferring again. That said, in every school she has attended, Xcaret thrives in all classes and shows great learning skills. Writing gave her access to escape reality when she felt the world around her collapse. To her, writing was just a hobby, and she never considered becoming a writer until Barrio Writers. Barrio Writers was an exciting summer activity which she will remember throughout her life and hopes to attend next summer. She is thankful for her mentors who encouraged her to use her voice.

Ink on Paper

I see trash bags filled with unseen objects
Trash bags that overlap pictures from books
It is just ink on paper
Until the ink becomes real and spills out
Now the trash bags overlap our streets
And pollution spreads
While violence erupts
From broken people
To tainted hearts
We blame God for the new terrors in the air
Yet we are the cause for our own fall
All because the ink on paper
Became our reality, spilled out

Dream House

Once upon a time, I had a dream about a forgotten house. It was far from civilization and noises. This house used to thrive and people from all over the world would come and enjoy its beauty. When you walked in, you were greeted with the sound of laughter, music, and clung to the smell of food trailing from the kitchen. There was a grand ballroom to one side were people danced and talked amongst each other. In front of you there was a large wooden staircase with detailed carvings and you could see people admiring the different rooms. One room was filled, top to bottom, with all sorts of plants and flowers. Vibrant colors flooded your eyes and vines wrapped around the sides of the room. In another room was a library, but not your basic straight column library. This library had books on spiral columns and books floating in the air, tied to strings on the ceiling. You could see people enjoyed these interesting designs. Some laughed at the fun architecture, while others conversed in deep thought, trying to figure out the reason behind the room. This house was loved by anyone who entered and left many in a dreamlike wonder. The house had no owner and was open to everyone who wished to see the famous "dream house". When everyone gathered around to eat, you could feel the warmth the house brought. People were not separated by race or religion and wars were forgotten, wrapping us in peace. The house was alive because the people gave it live. If you were to put you ear on any wall, you would hear a steady heartbeat. It was a beautiful sound. This was the dream house, the only place where walls brought people together instead of separating them. Then out of nowhere, shiny skyscrapers began to appear everywhere and technology advanced. Wars continued and people became distracted by TVs. People slowly stopped coming to the house until it was forgotten altogether. The walls lost its heartbeat, the books became coated with dust, and the once colorful plants shriveled up and died. The ballroom turned into a dark sulking area and the doors finally closed. This once lovely house filled with people became abandoned, miskept, and lost in a world of metal blocks and birds.

Who Am I?

I am Mexican American
From the roots of Santa Ana
I grew with the voice
Of those who crossed before me
Who gave their sweat and blood for me

I am my own person
From my parents' hard work
To their wishes for my success
With a mind that thinks for itself
But can never speak for itself

I am a woman
From the separation of men
Tied to old stereotypes
But fighting to change them
With a heart that beats for peace
I am me

Writing Activity

1."Ink on Paper" is an ekphrastic poem inspired by Lucio Muniain's "Are You Skeptical?" exhibition.

An ekphrastic poem is a dramatic description of a work of art. Ekphrastic poets describe drawings, paintings, sculptures, or life scenes. Ekphrastic descriptions can be realistic or imaginary.

Try writing an ekphrastic poem. Look at a drawing, painting, sculpture, photograph, or just look in front of you and start describing what you see. Describe how the art or scene engages your senses and what it makes you think of.

2. What is your "dream house"? Fold a paper up into eight squares. In the first square, draw a picture of the doorway to the house. In the next square, draw another room. Keep drawing different rooms for your dream house until you run out of ideas. Next, think about what the world would look like outside of your dream house. Write a story describing your dream house and how it would stand in the face of a changing world outside.

3. How would you answer the question, "Who am I?" Think about the people who have lived before you or raised you. How did they influence the person you are today? How does your culture and background influence who you are today? Write a poem answering the question "Who am I" describing yourself as an individual in your world.

Breana Lee

Breana Lee is 17 years old. She is a pure blooded Davisite who loves smiles, sunsets, and cereal, especially Honey Bunches of Oats. She aspires to meet the cast of "Captain America: Civil War" and Neil Patrick Harris, just to hear him say "Challenge accepted" in real life. She spends her free time baking, admiring art with bright colors, and watching the Food Channel. She is in pursuit of becoming a better writer, videographer, being updated on current news, and overall becoming a better person. She especially loves nature and hikes with bodies of water whether it be waterfalls, lakes rivers, or even puddles. She loves rain, but only occasionally. Her style is comfy, and she loves her dog Turbo more than words can describe. Most of all, she hopes for true happiness in her and everyone else's lives.

How long were you in prison?

Malcolm X entered the tiny bookstore early one summer day in 2017. It was humid outside and despite the sweat that beaded on his forehead, Malcolm X adjusted his tie and entered the store. He looked around at the stacks of books as the door closed with a soft twinkle of the bell overhead. The only person in the store was another mustached man standing in the Poem section, engrossed in a small paperback book.

The mustached man was standing, shoulders hunched, among the masses of books ranging from small pocket books to thick dictionary-like ones. Quietly, Malcolm X strode to the nearest pile of books and picked one up after lightly running his hand over the smooth spines. A golden flash had caught his eye. The Adventures of Samuel Thomas, Malcolm read to himself. This looks interesting, he thought. He flipped to the first page and began reading.

On July 9, 1892 Samuel Thomas was killed in an unusual accident near Cherry Hill. He was hit by an oncoming train moments before his final act. He was about to jump off the New River Gorge Bridge as a part of his one man show.

As Malcolm X continued to read, he was sucked more and more into Samuel Thomas' wild adventures. Malcolm X read slowly but persisted until he had read five full pages. He was still learning how to read quickly since his time in jail where he taught himself how to read and write using a dictionary. Closing the book, Malcolm X decided to read it later.

"What other kinds of books does this bookstore have to offer? Do they have any dictionaries?" He spoke aloud this time.

Looking up, he noticed the mustached man, with his attention still invested in the book he had been reading when Malcolm X first entered. Making his way over, Malcolm X picked up a book on the shelf at random. Startled, the mustached man noticed it was the same book he had in his hand.

"Do you like poetry?" the mustached man asked.

"No, actually, my favorite book is Merriam Webster's dictionary! Have you heard of it?" Malcolm questioned, excitedly.

"Yes, of course I have," the mustached man chuckled.

"It's how I learned to read and write with such flawlessness," Malcolm X joked.

"You probably saw me reading over there. I only got through 5 pages," Malcom X said.

"That's very impressive! What's your name young man?"

"Malcolm X," he responded extending his hand.

"Juan Felipe Herrera," the mustached man replied.

"Why did you choose to use a dictionary, of all books, to learn?"

"Well, sir, it was the only thing I could get my hands on in prison."

"Prison? What did you go to jail for?"

"Oh, just some of the civil rights rallies I was apart of," Malcolm X said off handedly.

"I'm about to go to get a coffee, would you like to join me?" Juan Felipe Herrera asked.

"Sure"

"Okay," Juan Felipe Herrera said.

"Let's call an Uber, oh wait I mean Lyft, we don't to support you know who," he decided, pulling out his iPhone.

"What is that? And I don't know who you are referring to..." Malcolm X responded, bewildered.

"How long were you in jail for?" Juan Felipe Herrera asked, laughing.

"We really do have a lot we can talk about," he said, as he exited the bookshop, Malcolm X eagerly trailing behind him to find out more about this shiny rectangle.

I wish I could be as fearless as a first grader

When we were in first grade the teacher would ask, "Can I have a volunteer?" and all hands would eagerly shoot into the air. They begin shouting, begging and pleading to be picked. "Me! Me! Choose me!" they all exclaim.

First graders are fearless.

They shout out, shove their fingers up their tiny nostrils, and climb everything without a care of what others think. They're willing to talk to anyone who's willing to listen about whatever's on their mind from their favorite zoo animal to the inner workings of their very own waterpark they invented.

When I was young, we were in New Zealand and visited Sky Tower in Auckland where we had the opportunity to do a Sky Jump, where, essentially, you jump off a New Zealand's highest building onto a green target waiting below. I wanted so badly to do the Sky Jump, reassuring my parents that I felt absolutely safe harnessed up. I was a little adrenaline junkie, I know. Unfortunately, I was one month younger than the minimum age and didn't get to do the jump. Looking back, I know I was a little crazy, but first graders are truly fearless.

Now in my senior year of high school, we're so full of fear that when the teacher asks for a volunteer, we sit in the all too familiar uncomfortable silence, waiting, hoping that someone will save us from the torture. Maybe, you could argue, no one knows the answer or maybe it's just the apathy of senioritis. Who knows.

But it can even get worse with adults in a public setting. Have you ever been to a speaker's presentation and they ask a question where no one's hand is raised? You'd be lucky if you got one.

What's conditioned us to hold back? We've all been trained to keep quiet, even if you know the answer or want to volunteer, the terrifying risks of what may happen if you speak up clouds all else. Something embarrassing might result and the destructive humiliation would be completely your fault because you choose to make yourself vulnerable. So who trained us? I think it's the rest of society. We've even been put down by other people and each traumatic experience has stuck with us, building up until it's as tall as that Auckland tower and each of these experiences has caused us to reconsider before putting our hand up again. When that hand goes up, you're also letting your guard plunge, defenseless to the unexpected.

I too am a victim of this fear. Asking me to willingly raise my hand or share private aspects of my life, thoughts, and feelings would be like asking me to hurl myself off a building. My desire to stay seated with my hands securely in my lap overcomes any desire or curiosity of what would happen if I volunteered. People will mock, judge, and disapprove of me. I'll end up making them see me in a worse than they did before, so I should simply keep quiet. I'll just see what happens when other people volunteer, I reason with myself. Those first volunteers take a huge risk, one that I am much too afraid of for my own good. I should get out of my comfort zone and speak up, but I just can't.

Those risk takers put themselves out there, vulnerability and all, helplessly on display but a lot of the time they reap its rewards. Free t-shirts or candy may be flung out into the crowds at school rallies but there I sit, quiet and composed, pretending to be un-phased and somehow better than the free prizes while the first grader in me wants to jump up and exclaim that I want a lollipop. The senior in me, though, drags down that first grader and sits her down forcefully. What will everyone think? the senior scorns. She only does this because she knows, from past experiences, that it may lead to disaster and she only wants to protect the first grader from harm. Disappointed, the first grader obeys and drops her eyes and with it her hope.

I know I should change because it's not a good thing to push down feelings in fear of what could happen, so I'll try to encourage that little first grader in me to overpower the timid senior because she deserves more credit than she gets for a 6-year-old. Let her push you, even if she has to shove you by the small of your back, out of your comfort zone because she is fearless and I think I can learn quite a lot from her and possibly get some of that free candy too. Maybe someday I'll even brave the Sky Jump.

Writing Activity

1. Do you recognize the characters in Breana's piece titled "How long were you in prison?" (If not, reread and locate the clues and google their names.)

2. Rewrite Breana's short story, here is the writing prompt: choose two other historical or iconic people you'd like to see in conversation who have never met or not from the same lifetime, choose a neutral surrounding (not a place associated with either of them) and they have to be in dialogue in the story.

3. In her second piece, Breana was exploring a topic for an "undergraduate essay" required for college applications. This was her creative draft—she focused solely on writing her experience then later adapted it for her college essay. Is there something you have overcome in life that can be a creative story then possibly adapted for a college essay? Try it!

Kimberly Phou

My name is Kimberly, and I am 14 years old. I like K-pop, such as the groups BTS, EXO, and Got7. My family consists of my mom, dad, and older sister. I am Chinese and Cambodian but born and raised in America. I've lived in Texas all my life. I'm not much of a writer but I always thought that those who wrote were cool because they can freely write whatever they want and people enjoy it. I think I'm able to spread my thoughts out more in writing than me actually speaking. My life isn't really interesting, but I'm happy with it. I'm happy with myself and what I am doing.

"Beauty" Under the Bridge

"Do you not see yourself? No man would ever love you!"

"If I liked you I might've felt pity towards you, but I don't, you're not worth THAT much."

"How can you live with a face like that? You must be stupid or foolishly confident."

Mei Yi Ran was the reason such words were said, as she was the maiden they were being said to. It was not a lie whenever someone would call Yi Ran's face "disturbing" or "grotesque" as it was true. Back in these days, it's normal to think that a woman who wasn't beautiful wasn't anything else at all except miserable. Yi Ran would be an exception though, as her heart was as kind as she was ugly. She was really "ugly". Many elders loved Yi Ran as the young bullied and teased her, including her ten beautiful sisters. Yes, beautiful they were, but their beauty was as strong as their hateful hearts, the opposite of Yi ran.

One night, as Yi Ran was fast asleep her sisters planned to get rid of her as they could not bear having her as a sister any longer, Yi Ran's face made them sick. They tied up and put a mask over Yi ran, they kicked and whipped her to unleash every ounce of hatred they had for her.

The sisters arrived at the Jade Bridge where the Jade Dragon lied, he was well known for granting wishes and loving all things beautiful. "O' Great Dragon we offer you our extremely hideo-er- I mean BEAUTIFUL younger sister!!" yelled the eldest. The sister's plan was to exchange Yi Ran to the Dragon in return for many more years of youth and anti-aging. The Dragon carefully examined the beautiful sisters and Yi Ran who was wearing the mask. "Very well," agreed the Dragon, assuming Yi Ran was as beautiful as her sisters, the dragon granted their wish.

"Stupid Dragon… WHAT A FOOL HAHA," snickered the sisters in unison as the merrily marched back to their home to celebrate the loss of Yi Ran and fooling the Great Jade Dragon.

Alone under the bridge, it was just the dragon and Yi Ran who was still wearing the mask. Frightened she spoke, "O' Great Dragon what will become of me now?" "I am going to eat you," answered the Dragon and he ate Yi Ran. Legend says that if the Jade Dragon eats something beautiful it becomes more beautiful himself, the legend was true.

Though Yi ran was not beautiful, she was still eaten… what will happen to the Dragon? The Dragon…EXPLODED! Its remains were changing into something different, a woman, a beautiful woman with a beautiful heart. It was Yi Ran. She, being eaten by the dragon, had become more beautiful as she was being digested. The dragon having eaten something not beautiful died, as his beauty and magic was absorbed by the kindness of Yi Ran's heart. Yi Ran couldn't believe what had just happened. She had become GORGEOUS AND SHE HAS MAGIC!! Yi Ran who was so very happy, got on her knees and apologized to the dragon "O'- Great Dragon I am terribly sorry as you have been fooled by my sisters… I shall avenge your death!" declared Yi Ran.

Yi Ran made it her duty to avenge the dragon's death, as it was because of him being gullible that allowed Yi Ran to change. Using the magic she had acquired Yi Ran placed a curse on her sisters, a curse that shall make their faces as ugly as they are in their hearts. It worked, they were ugly inside and out, the sisters were ashamed with themselves so one-by-one they each drowned themselves in the large well and died. Yi Ran didn't imagine her sisters would do something like that. She mourned all their deaths and cried. Yi Ran's tears eventually formed a stream under the Jade Bridge, her tears representing the life that awaited her, beautiful tears they were.

Writing Activity

1. Write a fairy tale that tells a story illustrating an important moral or wisdom for the youth of today. Include imagery, descriptions of characters and places, and dialogue.

2. Think about a time when someone made you feel bad about who you were. Write about how you processed that situation and your emotions that arose from that experience.

Briann Marie Allen

Briann Allen is an 18-year-old high school graduate from Pollok, Texas. She has lived most of her life with her grandparents and graduated from Central High School as the 3rd in her class. Briann will be attending Stephen F. Austin State University in the fall of 2017, and aims to obtain a major in Creative Writing.

Can You Hear Me?

Can you hear me?
As I whisper into the silence
No echo to reassure my presence
The empty is suffocating my
Claustrophobia is intensifying
Can you hear me?
I'm crying into the void I
Can't hear myself or my
Desperate attempts to create noise
There's nothing responding
Can you hear me?
I scream into this emptiness
But my voice is breaking my
Sound waves can't travel in a
Place of no medium I'm petrified
Can you hear me?
Can you hear me?
Can you hear me?
I will not be silenced any longer.

Effort

What do you know about me? How can you say these I am all these things if you've never tried to get to know me?

Your assumptions show your lack of effort. Lazy and unwilling to try, it will get you hurt. You'll say the wrong thing to the wrong person, and the consequences will hit like a Freight Train.

Don't conform to the lazy and assuming world, show a little effort. The discoveries you'll uncover with that effort will be more satisfying than sticking with the inferiority complex and hurting others to please it.

Be kind. Be rebellious. Be someone worth talking to.

This is Me

Bold, brilliant, bull-headed, blunt
Rhythmic, rational, reader
Imaginative, inquisitive
Amiable, accomplished, artistic
Nocturnal, nice, natural
Nervous
This is who I am. These are the words I believe suit me. You can disagree, you can try and correct.
But you don't know the true me from just the outside.

Writing Activity

1. Re-read the poem "Can you Hear Me?" How does Briann use repetition to add feeling to the poem? Think about a poem or essay you have written (or if you don't have one, start writing!) Would it improve your piece if you used repetition to emphasize a point?

Also take a look at how and where Briann chose to insert line breaks in this poem. Try reading the poem with the line breaks in a different place. Does it change the way you read it? How/why/why not? Spend some time writing a draft of a poem. Once you have it written, experiment with breaking the lines in different places and see how it changes the poem.

2. Look closely at "This is Me." This is what is called an acrostic. An acrostic is a type of poem in which the first letter of each line combines to spell a word or phrase, in this case, "Briann." Write out the letters of your name and try writing a "This is Me" poem in the form of an acrostic.

Next, try writing a haiku about yourself. A haiku is a type of Japanese poem that contains just three lines. The first line contains 5 syllables, the second line contains 6 syllables, and the third line contains 5 syllables again.Which type of poem do you prefer? Why?

K.J. Huey

K. J. "El Deafo" Huey was born January 8, 2002 to Patrick Huey and Dee Huey. She has one sister, Trinity Huey, and a half-brother, Austin James. She was born with nerve damage, which gave hear severe to profound progressive hearing loss but refuses to let that stop her.

I Blame; I Forgive:

I blame you for my pain. I blame you for my back then, my now, and my will be. I blame you for my anger, I blame you for my choices and their consequences. I blame you for time, even though time is a legend, a myth, a tall tale and I blame you for time being fake, a theory, a man thought thing. I blame you for death and its existence and I blame you for life, too. I blame you for life and death being fair and yet unfair all it the same instant. I blame you for butterflies and skeletons, death and life's ties to this world, their earthly symbols. I blame you for my mistakes and my lessons. I blame you for my mistakes and my lessons. I blame you for failure and for success; surrenders, defeats, victories, losses, stalemates-all because of you. My flaws and perfections are all the work of you. I blame you for my code and all of its virus; every time I malfunction is all on you. I blame you for my friendlessness and my phobias. I blame you for society and all judgments. I blame you for every lie spoken up or plastered down, and every truth is your fault, too. I blame you for my problems passed, my problems I now face, and all those to later come. I blame you for murder. I blame you for suicide. I blame you for sin and for all addictions. I lay all accusations on your shoulder for they are your responsibility and they are your fault. I blame you for hate, violence, bullying, and all forms of cruelty. I blame you for war and for peace. I blame you for debt. I blame you for forgiveness never received and apologies never given. I blame you for any and all wrong; every right is your cross to bear. I blame you for sacrifice, ungratefulness, and for unappreciation. I blame you for happiness, which never stays, and depression, which never seems to truly go. I blame you for all my tears and for my responsibilities and for my sweat. All blood is on your hands; you did this to us. You are the reason the sun never stays forever. You are the reason the stars are always afraid to shine. You are why the moon is the sun's mirror, for the sun must see you at all times. I blame you for darkness and I blame you for light. I blame you for evil and I blame you for good. I blame you for creation and the rapture. I blame you for Eve's weakness and the punishments that followed. I blame you, I blame myself. I blame the world for what's wrong and what's right. But God says not to blame so I let it all wash away by the rains of mercy and I dry off with the towel of grace. I forgive you, I forgive myself.

The Lord is Mysterious

What? What did you say? Where am I – oh, where am I from? Oh, I'm from the hearing world and I'm trying to escape. I'm deaf though, so I really don't belong there. My destination? Oh, I'm going to the deaf world. Makes sense, right? It's pretty far, though. It's in-it's in this universe but it's in the Galaxy of disabilities. How do you sit there? What? Get there? Oh, how do you get there? It's easy. First star to the left and straight on till midnight. I know, it is like the directions from peter pan, but Never-Neverland is in a different universe. Yeppers peppers, the Universe of Creativity in the imagination Galaxy on the Dream Planet. And it's that way, to the right. You're going left, too? Oh, they think you're crazy? People used to think the same of me, too. Not anymore. They're sending you where? Moon of Mental instabilities? Because they think you'll fit in there? Oh How very mentally unstable of them to say that. they're going with you too, right? No? Those mother butlers! Little twits. Huh? Oh no, I'm sick of the hearing world. They are so arrogant and negative. I want to go. You know, see what I've been missing out on my whole life. My dad is deaf also, but he wants to stay in the hearing world. Hmm? Oh, I'm going to be attending school in the deaf world. It's not just a world for only deaf people. People wanting to learn our languages, study our culture, be a part of the deaf world, friends, family, and acquaintances of deaf people live in the deaf world. You know what? Come with me. Please, I insist. We are acquaintances and I'm inviting you. It will be better than where you're going, I promise. Just stay awhile and if you don't like it you can leave anytime. I think you'll like it tough. Well, would you look at that? Some dude is walking over and I'm pretty sure he was checking me out. Oh, hello, sir. Did you come over to talk to him or to me? To me? What? What do you mean, "What him?" Yes, there is, he's sitting right – hey, he's gone. Maybe...maybe he went to the restroom. Wait... What? There was never anyone there? Oh...Loneliness does that to you. Plays tricks on-on your mind and...just...gives you someone to talk to sometimes. Thing is...I feel like that was Jesus I was just talking to. I mean, people thought he was crazy, too. They outcasted him and only a few people believed in Him. It would explain the sudden disappearance and why I could see Him. Jesus did many miracles when He was a person. Still does even though He's a spirit again. And no, I am – I'm not crazy. I mean, I used to think I was schizophrenic, but then I realized it was all Biblical. Every last bit. What's that? Say again? Please be patient, I'm deaf. You...you know sign language! You know my language! Huh? Tell you more About what? God? Gladly. Hey, you know these miracles I was talking about earlier? I think this is one of them. God sent you to me, so now I'm not lonely anymore. At least not for the rest of this journey, hopefully. Oh, uh, who are your friends? They want to know more about God and His only Son Jesus, too, huh? Well, I'm happy to tell. Wow. The Lord is Mysterious! There's twelve of you and there were twelve disciples. One me and one Jesus.

I have a Bible with me though. Jesus didn't have one, they didn't exist after His body died. I think. Anyway, let's get started. This trip is pretty long, so I'll start in the book of First John. That's where one of my pastors had me start when I was first saved. Saved? I'll talk about it later. It comes up in the Bible many times. Feel free to ask questions as I'm reading and I'll answer to the best of my ability. First off, let's pray. Dear Lord Heavenly, Father, I pray in Jesus' name…

What does it feel like to be you in today's U.S.?

Oh, it sucks. I'm a hermit with no life and no friends. I found out not long ago that it's highly possible that I'm autistic, which would explain a lot. It's hard to be deaf, so adding autism to the equation would make it even harder. The world laughs at autistic people and make memes that are slander, they make fun of deaf people just the same. People ignore me. It's like they're saying, "Oh, well, if she can't hear us we aren't going to hear her," as if it's my fault for being born with nerve damage and like it's my fault for deafness being hereditary in my family. They treat me as though it's my fault I have trouble communicating with people. "Oh, well, if she won't tell us stuff we won't tell her anything until the last minute." Because it's all my fault, right? I deserve the blame for everything right? NO!

Writing Activity

1. Take on the persona of "you" in "I Blame; I Forgive:." Respond to the speaker's accusations of blame. Are you to blame? Why or why not?

2. The speaker in the piece "The Lord is Mysterious" is trying to illustrate what it is like for a deaf person to talk with a hearing person. The writer repeating questions he/she has just been asked and asking for clarification on statements can be difficult for someone speaking with the writer, but when we think more deeply, we have all had difficulty understanding or being understood by others. Think of a time when you didn't understand something being explained to you. What happened? Did the person seem frustrated or angry with you when you didn't understand immediately? How did you feel?

Grecia Peñaloza

Grecia Peñaloza currently attends Century High School in Santa Ana, CA. The 17 year old dreams of going to college after high school. Although she isn't sure what she wants to be yet, she does know that she wants to help and influence others. Grecia enjoys sharing her personal stories with others in hopes that they can make a difference in someone else's life. Her free time is spent reading books and eating cake.

Noche

Una noche me cambio la vida completamente
En una noche de lluvia mis ojos vieron lo inesperable
En esa noche mis ojos vieron la infidelidad
Y desde ese día todo cambio
Yo perdí la confianza y obtuve inseguridad
Yo perdí la amabilidad y obtuve odio
Yo perdí el amor y obtuve rencor
¿Cuándo uno obtiene algo nuevo, no debería ser positivo?
Excepto ahora mis ganancias son negativas y tristes
Yo perdí a la persona que era antes
Ahora soy alguien que nunca quise ser
Prefiero perder lo que ahora eh obtenido y volver a obtener lo que un dia perdi

Sin El

Una paloma sin sus alas no puede volar
Un perro sin sus patas no puede correr
Un pintor sin sus útiles no poder pintar
Un nadador sin agua no puede nadar
Una niña sin la atención de su padre no puede amar
Y si puede amar, no será por mucho tiempo
Al momento que le rompan el corazón, ella se acordara de su padre
Su padre al que no le tiene confianza para contarle lo que pasa
Y la niña pensara que el primer hombre que le rompió el corazón fue su padre
¿Como amara y confiara la niña en otro hombre si en su propio padre no puede?
Si una paloma necesita sus alas para volar
Yo necesito la comprensión, atención, y amor de mi padre, para poder amar

Writing Activity

1. Grecia wrote an introduction in English but chose to write creatively in Spanish. Why do you think this decision was made? Do you speak differently and/or other languages for different purposes? Write a poem in English, then in Spanish. What did you feel? What was different? Explore the possibilities of every language you can! It's what poetry is for.

2. Grecia wrote a beautiful poem where she compares someone without their father's love like being a dog without legs or a dove without wings. These are similes. Write a poem using similes, comparing someone without love to animals without their features.

Clarissa Camacho

Clarissa Camacho is a 17-year-old Chicana activist, indie film enthusiast, alternative music fanatic and lover of all things morbid. She has dreams of taking down the patriarchy and becoming a leader in the community. She also one day hopes to attend school in Sweden and live out the rest of her days traveling the world with her pet fish, Sushi.

Screams

blistered lips and a blotchy complexion
a purity and youth stripped away at the hands of capitalism
humanity swallowed as a whole, with the false perception, that darker pigmentation is unworthy.
knee brace and fungal infections
human beings or property?
does darker skin equate sexualization?
plump lips and spider web veins
it seems as if hazelnut skin implies consent to men
as if screams and cries are of no value?
pleasure and fetishization is achieved
at the expense of innocence
leaving monsters
where only nostalgia and angels should be found
ample breasts and wide hips
my skin does not answer for me

Voices

little girl
you are strong
they chant
but as i sit in a pool of my own blood
in a body i no longer distinguish as my own
i cant help but feel a creeping isolation, a sickening weakness
that has split my temperament in half....
perhaps my livelihood has disappeared as well,
along with my will to live
you are strong
they chant
and the voices converse in my eardrums

as i wipe the trickling blood off my inner thighs
the demon feasted on morality
devoured my adolescence
sucked up my disposition
and released a toxicity
that ultimately
consumed my vitality
little girl
you are strong
they chant

Writing Activity

1. Clarissa isn't afraid to point out the injustices she sees in the world through her poetry. What do you see wrong with the world? Write a poem listing what you see wrong in the world.

2. Who is speaking in the poem "Voices?" Is it someone finding strength in another person? Who do you find strength/inspiration from? Write a poem where you are speaking to the person who inspires you/gives you strength.

Kaiss Robles

Kaiss Robles participated in the 2017 Barrio Writers summer workshop in Santa Ana, CA.

Nuestros Ojos

Esos ojos,
esos ojos de desolación, tristeza, y furia
esos ojos han visto la lenta y dolorosa muerte de un carnal

Esos muchachos de barrio,
buscan con desesperación un lugar donde sienten pertenecer
buscan un hogar
buscan amor,
porque su padre ya encontró su amor en la botella y su madre en la prostitución

Esos ojos,
perdieron su pureza al ser arrostrados por las calles

Las calles,
nos arrancó nuestra juventud . . . más bien nuestra inocencia

Las calles,
nos tenia como su esclava
lentamente destrozando nuestro ser mientras se reia en placer

El barrio,
a unos los ahogo en su miseria
otros logramos escapar

Yo soy unos de los que logró escapar,
ahora y por tiempo indefinido brillaran mis ojos con fuerza.

Pence

Dear VP Candidate Pence,

Let me remind you that I am not the only 'mexican thing' who carries resiliency magically, these so called "illegal aliens" are my hermanos and hermanas who have and always will make this country great

I am that 'mexican thing' who is a product of an alcoholic father and sexually abused mother

I am that 'mexican thing' who attempted suicide at the age of 14 and survived it

I am that 'mexican thing' who has fell into the never ending hell of drug addiction since the age of 13

I am that 'mexican thing' whose anxiety and depression make me question my value, my purpose, and whether or not I am going to make it through another day

I am that 'mexican thing' that regardless of these obstacles and being labeled broken, useless, and failure ... I proudly carry resilience en la frente!

I am that 'mexican thing' who is eternally rooted in paving the way for future xicanitas

I am that 'mexican thing' who works two jobs, volunteers with our child abuse center and volunteers as a sexual assault crisis counselor by night

I am that 'mexican thing' who doesn't let my abuelos' efforts go in vain. I AM the embodiment of their american dream!

Brown Love

you,
brown eyes
piel canela
mixed with;
pac's thirst for knowledge and better tomorrow
and maya's soft yet passionately persistent soul

you,
walked into my life in all your brown boy magic glory ... re-awakening the mujer I was before I lost myself in this world's bitterness

you,
revived the powerful, passionate, and poetic chingona in me

you,
are deserving of love, soul burning passion, tenderness, warmth, mind provoking books, and unforgettable adventures

you,
are poetry
from the way your beautiful brown eyes meet mine to the electrifying feeling
when your hands run through these curves that crave to call you home

you,
inspire me, together we are poetry

Abuela

hace 68 años la luna, estrella, y sol se alinearon para dar a luz al alma más bella que a caminado por nuestra tierra

hace 20 años recibí el universo en tu tierna caricia

hace 20 años que se sembró un amor inquebrantable

hace 20 años que una pequeña recibió el mayor honor y privilegio que es ser tu nieta

y 20 años que tú amor me alimenta, tu compasión me fortalece, y tú sabiduría me sostiene.

Mi refugio,
mi santuario de amor,
mi maestra de la vida
te amo cada día más.

XICANA

She is a juxtaposition of ganas, ache, dreams and resiliency

Her passion and courage are rooted in the air and love that creates the healing our ancestors have been needing for generations

We aren't from here nor there, we beautifully carry the struggles and diversity of the motherland and american dream

Perdonar

'y quizás nunca lograre perdonarte' son las palabras que reciñan en mi mente
al oscurecer

y quizás nunca lograre perdonarte porque al decidirte a subir tras el sobre
delante consumido por alcohol me robaste al tener un padre por siete años

y quizás nunca lograre perdonarte porque al abrir tu boca van volando insul-
tos, groserías, blasfemia que aterrorizan mi ser

y quizás nunca lograre perdonarte porque cada vez que hablo con un hombre
veo tu reflejo en sus ojos,
dejan mi alma acalambrada
dejan mi alma incapacitada
para amar, gozar, y triunfar

y quizás nunca lograre perdonarte simplemente porque no quiero,
simplemente porque no quiero.

Writing Activity

1. In "Nuestros Ojos," Kaiss explores the perspective of a community through the community's language. Think about your own community. What language is used there? What words, phrases, or sounds do you typically hear? What sights do you typically see through the eyes of your community? Write a poem using the language of your community to describe your own perspective or the perspective of your community.

2. Think of a politician, musician, artist, actor, or other famous person you have a message for. What would you like to say to them if you met them? Write an open letter expressing your message to them. Try to create a dialogue with them based on something they have said or done in the past.

3. What does the "American Dream" mean to you? Is it the same or different from the "American Dream" of your parents and your family? Write a poem describing what the American Dream means to you. Focus on how your dream is unique, how your dream is similar to others, and how your dream differs from those who came before you.

AVK

AVK is a second-year Barrio Writer struggling to produce an honest arrangement of what they want in his work. They want to make music for anyone who finds it difficult to live in fear of judgement. AVK has been producing music with FL Studio from his laptop at home. However, they wish to properly learn how to mix and compose tracks by hand. AVK also finds joy in photography and composing images from music. AVK has used hip hop as a means of motivation out of depression and uses it as a tool for learning and growing.

I Hate You (A Letter to the Author)

I seen you reflect in every stranger's eyes I meet
Untouched by milky white water
caught in a padded prison
I see you stutter and shake
I see you run back in the crystal pond's clear colour
I see you cower from friends in their prisms
So quick to be relieved of your shadow,
so jaggedly shaped
They won't need you again
after the grandfather strikes the second of his crucifixion
So might as well forget those rose tainted laughs
The old wood burning smell lingers
as the fantasy land remains as that,
a fabled valentine's vale
I know you're lost
trying to reveal a truth that isn't yours
You hang,
choking,
by the people who hurt you most
But they'll never know you like I know you

As for me, I hate you
But I love your vessel
So I'll keep you living as long as I can.
Consider me a damning tourniquet from doubts and fear.

Sincerely, the man in the mirror,

HOPE

system of Rooks

remembrance is something I've always found difficult
to embrace and hold is harder
than faking a stoic stone plated face
to never break or change
only fade, as forest winds harrow rocks
the tick of the tide gnaws away at my cliff side
clawing at the door as the fort knocks
Doomed to one day fall forward into that bore's drop
as this statue once locked To Time is laid to rest
in a grave of its own kind

Martyr's Place

To strike or kick a captured bull and think
this red cover's the cause of his anger
Pull a flag from out in front of him
and you get shanked
He smells that human blood.
You thought he'd sank back when you pierced his heart
You'd thought he pray to Lord
when he caught your sword
He saw that red cover and ran
then collapsed
As they stopped applauding when they saw your body

Evening

Somewhere's a reservoir still with wilted sunrays.
Somewhere's a reservoir still with wilted sunrays.

Illuminated under moving trees
there's some days its leaves part
To pierce the hallowed silence
left behind a mouth of bleeding tree bark.
Doomed to gluttony the feeds off its branch,
The dying river, through gulps and roars,
it drinks and shivers then tears the cold roots off the bank
Diamonds glimmer for its tired friend
as the rye withers

Rhymes slither from their page and sink as they lie disfigured
Daylight blank again as I try to paint pictures with red toxins

Somewhere within me is a reservoir holding sunrays
And when its leaves part I'm left with dusk
as the night starts
My mind parts; I fear sleep,
Scared to think of dawn.
The promise of a new day
The hope that might not come.

Follower

Have you ever thought about a world
where everything is exactly the same…
Except you don't exist?
Everything functions perfectly without you…
Ha, ha…
The thought terrifies me.

Time, I thought, would help my problems
They say it mends a broken heart,
stomach aches, and paper cuts
I was said to be fine
Just a little scathed and sad
But otherwise okay

Time, I thought, would help my problems
More time alone
Was what I thought I wanted
But I quckly found
That the more time you spend in a realm outside of your own
the more effort it put into mending itself
and the better you're forgotten

Time
was interrupted
but never broken
My friends
Hoping I'd come back
Were supposed to save me
But time made them happy

And they forgot
And my parents
Mom and dad
Just left

I hope they're not worried

Writing Activity

1. Take a moment to look in the mirror. Who do you see? What feelings and images arise? What would you like to tell the person in the mirror?

Write a letter to yourself describing who and what you see, feel, hear, and smell and a message for the person in the mirror?

2. In "system of Rooks," AVK explores elemental metaphors to describe like ocean tides, forest winds, and stone cliffs to describe feelings, actions, and identity.

What elements would you use to describe yourself? Write a poem using different elements like wind, water, earth, and fire.

3. In "Follower," AVK begins their poem with dialogue from a video game. The beginning dialogue serves as inspiration for the rest of the poem.

Try looking for inspiration in the words you hear in your life. Start a poem with words you have heard that interested you for some reason. Do the words make you think about some new idea? Do they make you laugh or feel a strong emotion? Do you simply enjoy the sounds of the words themselves? Write about how the words inspire you.

Nathaniel Lopez

Nathaniel Lopez is a Mexican male who is currently living in McAllen, Texas. He is about to be 15 years old this weekend, and he is a shy person. His favorite sports are football and soccer. He has been playing football for five years and soccer for one year. He hopes to soon go to college and play football for UT.

Stereotypes

I am a Mexican in this world that has been stereotyped by many people some people say I won't make it far in life but I believe I will, there just trying to put me down some people can also say mean things like "You don't belong here you belong in Mexico with all the other Mexicans" but that's because people in this world will put things in other people's heads that make them think this way like our great and powerful president Trump or the news man some of us wake up to in the mornings and see on their TV. Saying things like Mexicans are rapists or another black man shot down by a police officer why can't we just all love each other and get along not worrying about somebody's color, religion, or wealth wouldn't that be a greater America.

From Father To BEAST!!!

My father was a good kind caring man like any other good dad he loved his children until he changed and joined a gang then became addicted to drugs.

He changed when the drugs hit the brain

He changed when he helped in a shooting and came back home like nothing telling no one saying he was fine

He changed when I saw him get as skinny and pale as a skeleton with a crackhead he loved for who knows why there was no good in her he married her and I was supposed to call her my step mom

He changed when I saw pounds of weed in his garage and I pretended those were just beautiful plants to make him think a certain way but I knew what they really were

He changed when he wouldn't eat or sleep for days because instead he would rather smoke all night

But after all this I still miss him and forgive him for what he did all these years I would try to tell him "STOP" but when I did it would go in through one ear and come out the other he would just push me away and tell me "I am OK son just don't become me" but what was he a Beast I would cry sometimes and try to hide a blunt from him and throw it out when I could but that was nothing he had an army of them in his room whispering in his ear "Light me one won't hurt" but one became five and five became ten then to many to count. The BEAST is currently being held in a cage till he becomes human again so he can come back into my arms and love me again in the future. This was not a hate poem about my father it was simply just what he was at the time and what I want everyone to get out of this is gangs won't give you protection or power and drugs don't make you cooler or smarter so I want everyone to make a positive change and dad's love every second that you have with your kids like they're a beautiful plant that you created THANK YOU.

Writing Activity

1. In his first piece, Nathaniel considers President Trump's slogan "Make America Great Again" and what it means to marginalized communities who are most affected by discrimination and violence. How can you reimagine the meaning of this slogan to empower a community you belong to rather than to create fear?

2. A stream of consciousness poem or story means that you free write your thoughts on paper with little to no punctuation. Write a piece using this style about something that is important to you.

3. Have you known someone in your life who underwent a dramatic change? How did this change effect you? What do you wish you could have said to them?

Isabel Garza

Isabel Garza is a 16-year-old teenager who was born in Corpus Christi, Texas, on July 12, 2001. Isabel is the only female out of eight children, and is expecting her ninth brother in October. She goes to Roy Miller High School with her younger brother Thomas Jr., aka, T.J. Isabel currently plays the violin. She is starting her junior year this fall. Isabel likes to write fantasy and science fiction, but mostly fantasy. She is currently writing a novel called The Lady of Winter.

Dreams Come Alive

Every night, my dreams come alive
From magic to robots taking over the world
I live it
With every dream
I give it birth in my chicken scratch hand writing.
Let my stories be about
History
Resurrection
Death
Stars
Humanity
Love
Revolution
The Universe
Prophecies
Let them come alive.

The Lady of Winter

The click of heels and stomps of boots rang throughout a large hallway decorated with snowy whites, fall oranges, reds, and yellows, warm ocean blues, and springy pinks, violets, and greens. It was strangely, a chaotic beauty.

In the front of the group, walking, was a young woman of nineteen, who wore a pure white ball gown with beautiful lace sleeves that flowed over her hands. Fur covered her shoulders and back as a cloak dragging behind her. Her skin was pale; her frame delicate, almost like glass, but the woman seemed to not mind, for a gentle smile was on her natural pink lips. Whitish blond hair was up in an intricate bun, some strands, falling in her slightly narrow face. Light reflected off of a silver circlet with aquamarines on it. Cloudy ice blue eyes stared straight ahead, showing her blindness. She didn't seem to mind that either, for she walked confidently towards two large wooden doors.

The overly large doors slowly opened, and the woman practically glided in, the room filled with men and woman wearing assorted colors related to the seasons fell silent, with respect. As she passed, they bowed or curtsied. Climbing up four steps, the important female sat on a pure white and ice blue throne.

"Let us begin the trial," she said, her voice soft yet cold. Next to her, sat a male on a red and orange throne. His suit matched his throne, fading from red to yellow. His amber eyes shifted to her resting form, before shifting to his right, where another male sat. His throne was yellow and blue matching his season. A green suit covered his body. He glared at anyone who met his gaze.

"Lord Autumn, are you done staring at me, or are you going to say something?" The male turned to his glare to Lord Autumn, who glowered.

"My apologies, Lord Summer, I was wondering if you were done scaring the court so we can get started." Lord Summer was about to jump up, when a hand landed on his arm.

"Now, Lord Summer, I'm sure Lord Autumn didn't mean any harm, right, Lord Autumn?" Lady Spring looked at Lord Autumn, her light green eyes, glowing softly under the light of the courtroom.

"No, Lady Spring, I did not."

"Are you three done acting like children? The trial is about to start." Lady Winter turned her head towards the three rulers of the Season Court, who actually looked sheepish under her cold gaze. Coughing, Lord Autumn agreed.

"Yes, Lady Winter is right, the trial is starting. Bring in the accused!" The sound of struggling and cursing was heard as a male wearing red was dragged in.

"State your name and court."

"I am named Lysander, and I am a part of the Autumn Court."

"What are his crimes?" Lady Winter seemed to freeze the male under her gaze. Lysander froze, before he started to struggle against the guards holding him.

"During his human life, he murdered his own child, I guess that resentment stayed into his time in my court, for he tried to kill one of my younger members."

"He deserves to die. No one is allowed to live if they harm a child!" Lady Spring stood, glaring at Lysander.

"I agree, he could kill innocents. Most of my court members are children, so I will not let someone who hurts children live." Lady Winter also stood. Lord Summer stood next, and then Lord Autumn.

"It is decided, we, the rulers of the Seasons Court, sentence you to death. You will not go to the heavenly gates of Heaven, for you chose to join the court, so you will disappear, with no one to remember you. Court dismissed." Lysander was dragged away screaming, and the four rulers sat, sighing in relief.

Writing Prompt

1. Imagination is a key part of a writer's craft. They use it to build incredible worlds that allows readers to step outside world so they can come closer to their own. With a flash fiction piece, build a world unlike any other. It can be on a different planet, it can be about people having amazing abilities, it can have creatures, anything you want. Make it your own world and take us on a journey.

Adriana Galvan

My name is Adriana Galvan, and I am a Houston Barrio Writers 2017 participant.

Another World

In this time Mother Planet Earth has reached its full beauty and potential once again
Love, peace and happiness
There is no time and place for an ounce of hate
People are still dying, they're always going to die
The animals are united all and well and humans do not think twice of ever harming one of them
Ice exists on the poles of the Earth and surrounding oceans, sea life is all so alive and well
Flowers look more beautiful than ever just like all of the others
Everything is all under the control of peace and unity like it should be
I don't think I've ever been this appreciative of living itself and yes, it is very beautiful feeling I wish to discover one day because I know this dream will never come true

Writing Activity

1. Adriana's poem creates a utopia, a world where everything is perfect. Create a utopia in a poem! What is your idea of a perfect world?

Meagan McQuien

For starters, I was born in Hobbs, NM on April 3th, 1998. Any time have an issue of any kind, my family blames it on me not being a native Texan. How dare I. Though I have always excelled at writing academically, I discovered my passion for writing after it was introduced to me by my junior English teacher. His influence helped me express myself as I coped with mental illness; he read my frantic emails littered with angsty poetry and narratives every night my senior year. It was nice having a fan and someone to tell me that I was a talented writer. My current works are centered around my experiences with abuse, being a part of the LGBT+ community, and mental illness. After I finish my current project, I want to write a children's book that presents themes of emotions, coping skills, and respect as well as featuring my artwork. I want to teach children the values that prevent abusive relationships and promote cooperative existence while also giving children fun and abstract imagery to engage with. Also, shout out to my cat, Stevie, and my mare, Consuela. I would highly suggest to everyone to include animals in their life; my lovely fur children have brought me a lot of healing.

I Fear Dark Places Feb. 18

Where was the light?
When I was tucked behind
A rack of coats and
Stood in line with a row of rainboots
Hidden,
because they were out of season.
Hidden,
because they were crusted in dirt.
Hidden,
because I wasn't quite right for the weather.

Where was the light?
When the crest of the sunset
Couldn't reach above
The solid brick walls
That lined the alley ways
Of the quiet historic neighborhood
Hidden,
where the windows of the houses didn't peak.
Hidden,
So no one could notice him "fixing me"...

but breaking me.

Where was the light?
When my stomach scraped against
The top of the rotting wooden gate
And startled scavenging birds
That landed where the bird of brighter colors sat
And started to pick the little bird apart
Hidden,
because the feathers and meat were gone.
Hidden,
because they kicked the bones over with dirt
Hidden,
because the bird could no longer make a sound

I.Fear.Dark.Places.

Who can attest to the life and death of those whose life is made in the dark where the witness are blind?

What is the word of someone who said they heard but could not see the wrong?

If the bird is made silent, it dies in the darkness…

I don't look at the Heaven's when the sun has
dipped below the line of the trees and the ground,
for while you boast of your witness to the
scatter of the cosmos and the pull of the moon
as it sways the waters and the winds slowly,
you don't dare say they were a
witness to the evil you can't see when
the homes, and the streets, and the allies
are hidden by the dark

When he's man, you look into the eyes of darkness too lightly.

The Minister Mar. 25

The Minister
He wanted to show me the love of God

and I was confused that saving me from
my lust for women had nothing to do with it.

He could care less for the
Bigots at the heels of the
Hooves of the glorious chariot horses that
Took disheveled judges to the mouth of God,
For so long as my heart was wandering,
His hands were bound to his guiding staff.

For me, He wanted that, guidance,
But I was a creature unlike Himself.
He loved something He could not understand.
He knew his staff could not guide me.

He brought another like me,
Perched Her where we could all see.
The non-creatures took her words,
Put them to their minds
And damned Her to a place beyond their Heaven.
I hid my heart beyond their Heaven too.

Thank God the Minister would meet me there.

Beauty ™ Mar. 30

"Love yourself", she says.
"You can be a sexy strong woman
Like me if you drink this
low cal, vegan, protein dense smoothie
because it will make you the beautiful
you can be!"

Why my eyes went
from the Vine star
to my stomach then
to my thighs then
towards the mirror into
the pupils of my eyes…
… She would say that she doesn't know why.

Thats what she was told to say

by the guy with the
camera in his hand
and the contract in her bank
because he knew that if he took a
hot button word and
used a woman to weave his gold
he could reach his goal
of being a millionaire by thirty
And in Forbes by sixty
While he called his spokeswoman sexy

And she's left to ask
If it was worth her time
To become the face to take
Beauty and make it Beauty ™
She sure doesn't get the royalties
from working to be perfect.

Writing Activity

1. Define feminism
a. If the writers don't know, have a writer look it up on their phone.
b. Ask the writers how they first came into contact with the word.
c. This may organically start a discuss of whether this word is good or bad, which is absolutely natural and what we want the writers to be thinking about. Empower their authority on the matter.

2. Define binary.
a. Put the definition on a large board or paper. Have the writers put this definition down in their own words.
b. Give examples on the board of some binaries, such as light vs. dark, men vs. women.
c. If the writers are timid, guide them to the fact that most binaries are a contrasting of good versus bad. Thus, what is on the left side is inherently good, and on the right, bad.
d. Let the writers discuss why this is and if this is fair or right.

3. T chart: Have the writers take a sheet of paper and draw a big T down the middle. On one side, have them write patriarchy and on the other matriarchy. Discuss definitions.
a. Have them write as many words as possible to describe each side.
b. Don't be surprised if they write situations or phrases like "man of the house."

4. Ask the writers to pick one item from either side and for the moment, write it at the top of the next clean page.
a. In any form (poetry, story, etc.) the writers should use this item to understand why this describes patriarchy or matriarchy.

5. Writing advisors can choose other words or leave the two words up for the writers to generate as long as the words are "opposites" of each other.

José Salvador Chávez Chávez

Mi nombre es José Salvador Chávez Chávez y tengo 10 años. Soy mexicano y me gusta toda la comida mexicana porque es muy sabrosa. Lo que me mas gusta de México es visitar a mis abuelos, y a mis primos porque ellos no tuvieron la oportunidad de venir al norte. Y me da tristeza porque yo quisiera que estuvieran en el norte porque me gusta jugar beisbol con mis primos. Y lo que no me gusta tanto es la música Regional Mexicana porque no me llama la atención. La música que si me gusta es trap y rap porque tiene muchas rimas.

Mexicanos y más mexicanos

Todos tenemos que luchar
contra la discriminación
tenemos que hacer que no hay más racismo
ni odio
no importa tu color
de donde eres
o como eres
tenemos que aceptar a cada humano,
tenemos que aprender que todos somos iguales.

Mi favorito día

Mi favorito día fue cuando nací,
fue el día que hice a mi familia feliz,
fui el primer hijo de mis padres.

Puedo imaginarme
que mima estuvo tan feliz
que quería bolar
y mi papa trajo mariachis.

Cuando tenga hijos
serán los mejores días de mi vida.

Writing Activity

1. José decided to write about his culture and in his first language. What culture do you identify with and what parts of it are you most proud of? Write a poem using the five senses (sight, sound, touch, taste, smell and maybe there's a sixth sense!) to describe your culture, feel free to write in your first or second language.

2. In his second poem, José was prompted to write about his favorite moment in life. As you can tell by his bio and writing, José uses humor in his work. For some people that comes naturally, is there a humorous story from your childhood or maybe more recent that can turn into a short story or poem? Just write it as you would tell it to your friends or family, don't worry about grammar or details being perfect.

Shaelyn Westbrook

Shaelyn Westbrook is a singer, writer, and babysitter who has been through childhood trauma. She constantly works to make sure that her voice is heard so that people know that they are not alone. Her writing tends to lean towards nonfiction and poetry that address major issues such as sexual abuse and suicide. She is a major enthusiast and protester for the LBGTQA+ community and plays an active role at her church, The Vineyard.

My Abby

Her eyes were the color of emeralds.
Her pale skin, brightened by them.
Her beautiful dark locks fell in curls down past her shoulders.
Her lips.
Oh God, her lips….
They were so full and red.
I miss every day that I'm not kissing them.
She never let me down.
My best friend. My lover. A large part of my world.
I never could understand how such a beautiful creature could hate its existence.
An angel, tortured. Forced to live in such a cruel and unloving world.
There are times where I can't even explain how she makes me feel.
I feel as though my heart is torn because there's nothing more that I can do.
I would die for her happily.
I would kill for her, guilt free
She's so far away from my arms and I yearn for her. I can no longer hold on to how I feel.
I love you and you will forever be mine.
My beautiful fallen angel.
When names and criticisms became too strong, she had an idea…
A shooter of Benadryl and heavy liquor is what gave my Angel her wings back.

Not Your Average Fairytale

In a world of pure and beautiful contrast to darkness.
No dreadful color lurks here, but all is not as seems.
A forest filled with pastel blues and greens and pinks, one's fondest dreams.
Passing through these trees is a girl and wolf, but this isn't the fairytale it

seems to be.
The wolf of white fur and tattoos weaving through the hairs stops to offer the little girl help.
This little girl, so pure and innocent obliges for directions.
As they walk the wolf offers her a flower as delicate as she.
Taken from his hands, the flower now firmly grasped in the hand of the child.
As they meet a fork in the road, the wolf bids fair well and safe travels to the girl, for this was his exit.
At that moment her pigtails resembled something of horns and her true self came to form.
She smiled mischievously, licked her pale chapped lips and her face bared grotesque and unsatisfiable hunger.
With jagged teeth she sprung towards the wolf and ate him with no remorse.
Appearances are deceiving, aren't they?

Writing Activity

1. In her poem "My Abby," Shaelyn shares her admiration for and sorrow for a lost love. Take some time to think about someone in your life who needs to know how much they mean to you and write a poem of elaborate, expressive, enthusiastic emotion to them (often referred to as an "ode").

2. In "Not Your Average Fairytale," Shaelyn ends a familiar fairytale with a "not-so-average" trick ending. Take a moment to remember a favorite fairytale of yours and write about it with a re-imagined ending that is also "not-so-average."

Aphra Ezar

Aphra Ezar has never liked writing author bios; he'd much rather be applying his skills to other projects—well, that and he's never written a bio he was satisfied with. A Nacogdoches native of mixed Polish, Jewish, Irish, and African heritage, Ezar (pseudonym of Alan C. Parr) aims to defy the traditional genre restrictions of contemporary writing. In public situations, it always offends me that certain people expect me to act 'ghetto' or 'black' when I'm not. It isn't like I'm the only one who goes through this—millions of mixed-race people across the country suffer similar discriminations, and I know quite a few who are scared to tell the truth about their ancestry because it's easier to conform to the expectations thrust upon us. Well, call me stubborn, obtuse, pigheaded, I don't care; I refuse to give the world that satisfaction. Only God can judge me.

"Just as I refuse to be labeled as a person, I wish to provide readers with original and thought-provoking works of art—writing that won't fit in any of the boxes they're familiar with. I feel that Elohiym has inspired me and given me this gift for a reason, and that that reason is to prove to the world that He can make a disciple of even the most desecrated of us human beings. So, I hope you enjoy these stories; just know they aren't just my own—they are the stories of us all."

Ezar has been telling stories since 2008. At the encouragement of English teacher Darius Tubbs and librarian Sonja Schulz (both under the employ of Nacogdoches High School), he joined the Barrio Writers 2017 Nacogdoches Chapter.

Human

Look at me.
Look into my eyes—
Eyes the color of earth—
And tell me what it is you see in them.
Look at my hands—
Callous, bronzed, and scarred.
My feet—
Oversized and hairy, with cracked yellow nails.
Heart—
Pumping blood as ruby-red as yours.
Mind—
A wish to be recognized individually,
And not a statistical anomaly.
I challenge you to look at me—
Not at my skin but my soul.

I challenge you to listen to me—
There's something that I need to say:
I challenge you to
Love me,
Because I am
Just the same as you:
Lost, confused, and in a dark and lonely place.
Because whether you like it or not,
We are of the same race—
Because we are both
Human.

Patchwork Quilt

Life is, I think, a patchwork quilt woven of dreams and memory,
And love's what gives the quilt its warmth: a gateway to eternity.

Faith is what holds the patches in place, ensuring they don't fall apart.
Pain tests the strength of thread worn thin but will in time make pure the heart.

Song breathes soul into the story; art gives color to the grey.
Each patch tells tale of a kindred spirit, with guidance of God to light its way.

Some say that is life like a flower, destined only to fade and wilt,
But I laugh at their close-mindedness and say that life's a patchwork quilt:

Sewn by none but the hand of God and passed from the hands of those afore,
This quilt's a treasure I'll duly cherish: my sail—take me to a distant shore!

Of Flight and Fall: The Earthbound Hawk (a different telling of Eden)

I HAD WINGS, ONCE UPON A VERY DISTANT TIME. They were my love, my life, my pride: the gold and rusty hues of the autumn sunset, as wide as the wispy cirrus and as potent as the thunderhead. I had no home but the sky. I had no family but the sun. I had no friend but the wind, no lover but to have my breath stolen in the rush of the dive. And I had no gods but my wings, twin bringers of battle and blood.

Oh, I was a vain creature, I realize now. I thought myself a king over all birds, a master of all the earthbound creatures of Eden. But I would be debased so that even the worms would mock me…

***

"Good-day, Hawk," an overly cheerful voice sang above the rain.

I groaned inwardly. "And what's so good about it, Sparrow? The skies are grey and my wings are soaked through—how can I fly like this?" I demanded, holding out my sodden feathers and spraying the little bird with water. "Unless you have a reason to be intruding upon my hospitality, then go away; this is my branch of my fig tree."

Sparrow, that patient and long-suffering ally of mine…he was the true hero of this story, I suppose, and I the villain. And, as in most stories, the hero received no justice.

"Well, I am sorry you're so down about it, but I personally am glad you aren't up in the air to-day. You're a much better flyer than me, Hawk; I won't deny so. It's only that you fly high, and I tire easily and am left below to watch only your silhouette emblazoned against the sun. Quite a majestic sight, but also very lonely for those you leave behind. I'll say any day you cannot fly is a good day for me, at least—days such as this are the only days we can really talk together anymore. Not like when we were both fledglings testing our wings in the undergrowth. Here," said Sparrow, pressing a sac made of dry leaves into my talons. "It's not much, but I saved you some breakfast."

I grunted morosely and shredded the bundle; the sugary aroma of papaya and blueberry rolled over my tongue. Trying not to seem too excited, I nodded at Sparrow in begrudging thanks before starting work on the meal. It was entirely too small, but looking back it must have been quite the burden for the small creature.

"I remembered it was your favorite," said Sparrow, whistling happily as he saw me lose my composure and greedily lapping every drop of nectar I could from the inside of the sac.

"Yes, well…" I cleared my throat. "You said that you miss talking. So, talk, or leave me to my own devices, please."

Sparrow blinked, and then looked around to make sure we were out of earshot of the other creatures. "Eve's catbird has moved on from her, and the queen of the Garden is looking for a new song-master. And so, I thought, well…if maybe I could ask the honor."

Before I could check myself, I laughed in the little bird's face. "You think to woo the godling? Oh, Sparrow, your song is sweet, but with such a sorry garb as yours Eve would never take you for her pet."

"It's true; I'm not much to look at, am I?" Sparrow looked down at his cloak of dull, sooty feathers, ashamed. "Oh, you're probably right, Hawk; you're right about most things. A silly dream..."

"That, Sparrow, is the difference between us: all my dreams occur during sleep."

"But…still, I want to try. Surely she will find some good in me."

"The queen of all Eden, who has the peafowl to fan her when she is hot and the magpies to bestow to her whatever gifts she demands—what have you, to compete with these things?"

"I've a kind heart, and I'm a hard worker. Hawk, old friend—"

"You are not," I snapped, stomping up to the little bird and looming over him, "any 'friend' of mine, Sparrow. You are an annoying, overly merry pest that offends the eyes and the ears. I don't know when you got the notion that we were ever close, but I suggest you put it from your mind, and quickly." The trembling bird looked as if he was about to cry, but I continued on irately, "You know, perhaps Eve might keep you on after all—as a comic, and her performing fool. Go, now, and find some other creature to vex." With that, I turned abruptly, sweeping my tail under Sparrow's feet and knocking him from the branch. He fell into a mud-puddle at the base of the tree.

"I don't know what's gotten into you lately," Sparrow half shouted, half sobbed from the ground. "It's all the fault of that nasty Serpent; you've been talking with him again, haven't you? Don't deny it! He's been turning the animals against each other, and I'm the only one that sees the damage he's doing! Well, you'll see eventually, you'll all see—and when you do, it shall be too late!" And with that, the little bird hopped away, limping slightly and dragging his tail behind him.

«Do you not pity the wretched little bird?» hissed a familiar voice in my mind. I craned my neck to see Serpent draped over the branch above me, watching Sparrow's departure with an unreadable expression in his eyes.

"No," I snapped, turning back—but Sparrow had disappeared into the rain.

Serpent chuckled as he slithered down the trunk to join me on my branch. «Well, in all honesty, neither do I. He is a weakling who forgets his place; he's no respect for his betters.»

"That's exactly what irks me about him—he admits himself he's no great flyer and that he's an eyesore, yet he thinks I would lower myself to be his friend. If only I were truly king of the birds, I would teach that Sparrow a thing or two about—" I clapped a wing over my beak and looked anxiously at Serpent, who regarded me with a hard glint in his red eyes.

«Treason. The Hawk speaks mutiny against the crown of Man.»

"No, you misunderstood me, Serpent; I only meant that—" I was cut off as Serpent laughed again. The sound, high and rasping, sent a chill down my spine and caused my feathers to stand on end.

«I like the way you think, young avian. Might I share a secret with you?»

"A secret? What is a secret?"

«Ah, the naïveté of all you mortal beings is refreshing. A secret, young Hawk, is a story only you can know, kept hidden from the eyes of others—and the secret I wish to share with you is that…I, too, wish to topple the crown.»

"What? You—"

«Let me finish, impatient bird; you would fly off into the monsoon without a second thought and have your wings torn off by the winds!» Serpent glared at me, and I clicked my beak shut. I felt some strange power emanating from the reptile's scales—angry and cold and dark and not in the least bit pleasant. «Yes, you do well to fear me, Hawk; I wield power you cannot imagine, and I have waited patiently—but now I have the strength to claim this world as my own.» He twisted his mouth into a fanged sneer. «Tell me, young Hawk…how would you like the chance to rule the skies above this Garden?»

***

You know this next chapter in my tale—how Serpent beguiled the wife of Adam, how he charmed her with his voice and seduced her with his eyes and the alluring movements of his body. How she in turn enticed her mate to sin. How the Man and Wife were forever banished from the Garden by Eloah, and cursed unto death, and how Serpent was cursed to crawl in the dust, winning the sympathy of most all the dwellers in of Eden. In the confusion that followed, Serpent became my teacher, and, though he could no longer himself hope to ascend to any great height in the world, he saw my wish fulfilled. I was crowned king of all avian life in the Garden. But, I too, would pay the price for my misconducts…

***

«Now, look at yourself, Hawk. All the flying creatures of the Garden tremble before you, and even Eagle bows her head and submits to your Will.» The sky was clear and still that day, and Serpent was sunning himself on a rock at the foot of my tree. I stood beside him, perched atop a root.

"Almost all, teacher Serpent. You forget that upstart, Sparrow."

Serpent gave me that dark look again, and I felt his voice ring inside my mind. «What is Sparrow to you now, my liege, but a minor annoyance? If he bothers you so, why not make him…disappear?»

I blinked, and, just for a moment, I remembered a time when—though I could never have admitted it—I had liked the little bird, all those summers ago when we were only fledglings and knew nothing of the world. But I looked into Serpents eyes, and that coldness seeped back into my heart. I thought I knew what that feeling was; I'd mistaken it for the feeling of power…now, all these winters later, I know its name as Evil. "And just how, pray tell," I whispered, "do you suggest I do this, Teacher?"

«Look to the fields. Listen. Watch. Something is missing.» Sighing in mild exasperation, I hopped from my resting place at the root of my tree to the branches, until I could see the sea of gold off to the distance. Sure enough, something was off, and it took me only a moment to realize what it was. The wheat was still—deathly still. I could hear none of the joyous chatter among the creatures that lived there; more than that, I could not even hear their heartbeats.

"Where have the mice gone, teacher Serpent?"

The reptile's hissing laughter carried a hint of madness as he said, «They have all disappeared…into my belly! Don't you see what power we wield, with Man gone and the law of Eloah broken? We control Death itself!»

"You ate them?" I asked, recoiling. I'd never heard of one creature feasting so on another. It was just…just wrong. Unheard of. We had all the food we needed, provided for us by the Garden. There was no need to…and yet…

«I did save one for you, young Hawk…if you were hungry?» A false air of innocence now surrounded Serpent. «I left it for you in a hidden place…I shall return shortly with a meal for you, O King.»

I couldn't believe I was even considering it, but by the time I had made it back to the ground, Serpent was gone. True to his word, however, he was soon back, dragging a bundle along the ground. «I assure you, it's quite fresh; the blood should still be warm.»

"I'm not sure that I needed to know that particular detail." I shuddered as I saw the bundle's contents. In my talons was a limp field mouse, its dark, glistening eyes staring up at me blankly. "How do I even…ah, that is…" I trailed off, unable to finish the question.

«Oh, that one's small enough that I imagine you could swallow it whole—but tear into the belly with your beak and taste him first; there's no drink like blood to quench your thirst.»

I flipped the poor thing over, squeezed my eyes tightly shut, and, before I could lose my nerve, bit down. Hot, salty liquid spurted into my mouth and stained my facial feathers a deep red. I threw the mouse to the ground and tried to spit the taste out of my mouth. "Bleurgh!! I was right when I thought that this was a brainless idea. Please tell me that this will wash out," I said, trying to wipe myself clean but succeeding only in staining my wings, as well.

«You don't like it?» Serpent sounded mildly disappointed.

"No, I do not; I think I might be sick…"

«The things that are beneficial to us often seem repulsive to us—that is the way Eloah rules, with lies and with oppression. But wait a moment. Once the blood reaches your stomach—» All at once, a fiery, empowering rush overtook my senses. My vision sharpened, and I could see every iota of dust floating lazily in the air. My hearing was likewise enhanced, and I could hear Serpent's stomach working as he digested his own meal of mice. The acidic tang on my tongue suddenly turned to honey. I snatched the discarded mouse back into my talons and began to devour it, noisily shredding and smacking until all that was left in my claws was a tuft of bloodied fur. «There. It would seem that the blood has taken effect.»

"How?" I marveled, watching as a sudden puff of wind blew the fur into the air and dispersed.

«You didn't really think a bird such as yourself was meant to live on berries and nuts? Not with those wicked talons. Not with that sharp beak.

«Hawk, don't you see? The strong are meant to rule the weak, and the weak are meant to give life to the strong. It is a balance, a beautiful, holy one… and Eloah has hidden it from you, out of fear that you would one day surpass Him in glory and power,» hissed Serpent. «Can you not see the harm this being would inflict upon us? Look what He has done to your teacher, merely for speaking his mind!»

"It's true, he has mocked you sorely. A shame, really—your wings were the pride of all the reptiles."

«And Eloah took them from me. But you—you have become my wings, young Hawk. I am indebted to you.»

"Don't flatter me, Serpent; I'm not as easily directed as most." I shook my head. "This conversation has gone awry. What were we speaking of? Ah, yes—what does the mouse have to do with my problems with Sparrow?"

Serpent looked at me blankly. «I would have thought the matter obvious.»

For a long moment, neither of us spoke. And then dread stirred inside my breast as I realized what it was that Serpent suggested. "Never."

«Well, why not?»

"I refuse to kill and eat an avian, even one as bothersome as Sparrow. How could you even begin to think that I would—"

«Young Hawk. Young, sweet, naïve fool of a bird. Have I ever given his Majesty unsound advice in the past? Did I not aid you in your ascension to the throne, even at the cost of my own ability? Trust me, my friend. I wish only to help you,» whispered Serpent in my mind, twisting his thoughts around my brain and constricting me. I could feel myself suffocating inwardly as I was caught in his hypnotic gaze. «It would be so easy to do; Sparrow is so weak. Why should he deserve to live in your kingdom? The strong shall rule the weak…»

"..and the weak shall give their lives for the strong." I said dazedly, fully inhibited by Serpent's spell.

«Yes. Now go, good Hawk, and pass holy judgment on your subjects.»

"I…shall return," I mumbled, my thoughts foggy, my vision out of focus. I spread my wings and took to the air, riding the westbound winds to where Sparrow's home was.

Sparrow's nest was in a little shrub on the outskirts of the Garden. The little bird seemed to have become rather introverted; unlike the other nearby nests, which were constantly being tended to so as to discourage the growth of weeds, the entrance to Sparrow's was blocked by a growth of thorns.

"Is anyone at home?" My voice sounded odd even to myself, and my tongue moved of its own accord; I had lost all sense of self, my body merely responding to Serpent's promptings, still whispering in my mind.

«You want to seem amicable. None can know of your true intent.»

Whose true intent? The thought struggled to surface from beneath the murky sea Serpent had made of my head—what am I doing here? Have I come to finally make amends?

«NO!» Serpent's voice exploded in my head, causing me almost to fall over.

"Lord Hawk?" A peep came from behind the wall of vine growth. "Is that you?" The little bird shambled into the clearing, forcing his way through a gap between the brambles. "Why have you come here, my…my liege?"

"I'm not entirely sure," I said, shaking my head, trying to clear the haze. "I don't feel quite myself…I haven't felt like myself in a very long time."

«You are here to punish the one who has affronted you.»

"Your feathers are so red…did you become overly enthusiastic while eating cherries again?"

"I remember that!" I laughed, before Serpent's anger slammed into me with the force of the raging Tigris, and I crumpled to the ground, moaning softly.

"Hawk, what's wrong?! Are you sick?"

"Only of your blathering tongue," Serpent spat, using my voice. "You are the one creature that stands between Hawk and his sole subservience to me."

Sparrow jumped back, his dark eyes wide with fear, his feathers standing on end.

"I whispered in Hawk's ears, making him resentful of you, his first and only friend. He's always been convinced that you're somehow a more moral being then he is—I used that against him, snaring his heart with hate without his knowledge. If were one to compare your hearts by Eloah's standards, I suppose you would be the better bird," Serpent said, and my body obeyed his command to raise my wings and block Sparrow's escape, "because now Hawk is going to kill you." And with those words echoing in my ears, the world around me spiraled into utter blackness.

***

When I came to, lying splayed on my back in the clearing, it was just before sunset, and it had begun to rain once more. The sky above was the color of blood, and all around me I heard confused and mournful whispers. One voice, one I was all too familiar with, rose above the others.

«Here is the one you have crowned your king, feathers stained by blood that is not his own—and where is poor Sparrow? Poor, sweet, innocent Sparrow is gone from the world, save for the single feather hanging in Hawk's gluttonous maw!» Serpent's voice cracked. «Oh, what devil have we allowed into our midst?»

"What has happened?" I asked, voice raw as if from screaming. "Why am I on the ground?"

«What has happened?» Serpent wailed. «The murderer, the eater of his own avian brother, feigns innocence even as the blood is washed from his feathers and pools at his feet!»

"Murderer? I do not know the word," I said, hoisting myself on shaking legs up and blinking the darkness from my eyes. I looked around; I was surrounded on all sides by wide-eyes creatures of all the kingdoms: Avian, Mammalia, Reptile, the list went on. It seemed all the inhabitants of Eden were staring at me, and I had no idea why. At the front, slithering back and forth and staring at me accusingly, was Serpent. "Teacher? Wh—"

«I am no teacher of yours, Hawk,» the snake spat, glaring at me with his red eyes. «Now, cease your foolish games. We have been to your tree; we saw the bloodstained bones of the field mice hidden in the knothole. Admit to your crimes, and we may yet let you leave us freely. Admit to us that you are the one who took Sparrow's life in your selfish anger and that you are the one who spilt his blood for sport!»

All at once, I remembered everything: how Serpent had coaxed me into eating the mouse, and how he had then bewitched me, and took control of my body, and—

It was too much. I sank to the ground once more and vomited, and the mangled and partially-digested corpse of a small bird spilled out of my mouth.

«The final proof,» hissed Serpent, a trace of smugness reserved exclusively for me entering his voice, «now lies before us, brothers.»

"Let us kill him now, before—"

«No, Lion! Would cause more death than has already transpired on this night?» Serpent seemed close to tears, but I saw the evil in his eyes and knew for the first time his true nature.

Devils cry for none but their own, and this pawn had outlived his usefulness.

***

The rain swelled to a monsoon, and while the other creatures of Eden sought shelter, I was forced to flee into the air. Ironically, Serpent's admonishment proved true; my left wing was severed from my body completely, and my right now dangles uselessly at my side, attached by a thin rope of sinew. The worms laugh at me even as I scratch through the dry, cracked land in this desert country where I have been carried. I eat nothing but weeds and drink nothing but the morning dew, every day screaming silently, begging forgiveness that I feel I will never receive.

Amen.

Writing Activity

1. The author in the first piece takes an honest look at his physical appearance. What are some things about your physical appearance that make you concerned people won't want to get to know who you are on the inside? Write about how those things are a part of who you are, but do not necessarily define who you are.

2. Write about some of your experiences and memories in a poem or prose format that creates a picture of who you are and where you come from.

3. How have good and bad experiences and memories made you the person that you are right now? Compare and contrast a good and bad experience and how it influenced who you are today.

Stuart Olson Beal

Stuart Olson Beal is a slightly obnoxious (many would argue he drop the slightly), definitely loud, and constantly talkative 14-year-old boy living in Nacogdoches, Texas. He enjoys playing the piano (shout out to his man Debussy for composing the sweet tune he's working on now), playing the trumpet for his school's band (wait, this is a list of things he enjoys…), dancing at the Gobel School of Dance (he unfortunately has no sarcastic comment for this one), swimming on his high school swim team (breaststroke is where it's at, guys), and reading books (mostly Stephen King and cheesy but thoroughly entertaining young adult novels). He loves his family a whole lot but can't wait to be an adult and live in Portland, Oregon with three corgis.

My Voice is My Weapon

My voice is my weapon and although this may be true,
mine is dull and unused and yours is too.
We never pull out these weapons and use them to fight,
because no one needs us and our unexperienced and youthful might.
You may deny this truth but look around,
the youth of this nation are lost and not yet found,
We're confused and we quite often make bad choices,
because we've been locked into cages and robbed of our voices.
Contrary to what you might think we have tons to say,
we just refuse to say it or think it in what might be considered your way.
So let us stand up and talk and confuse you,
It will make us happy and just might change your views too.

The Cautious Boy in Crocs

One moment, one second, and I'm there. The place where my dreams always take me. I'm standing outside the airport with beautiful Icelandic scenery surrounding me. I take a minute to breathe in the cool, crisp, clean air and admire the thin layer of fluffy, white snow that has covered this barren landscape around me. Behind me is the Keflavík airport, the hub of air travel for the entire island of Iceland. Its glass walls reflect light and warm up my back offering a short respite to the harsh, cold wind that is easily cutting through my thin SFA T-shirt, my nerdy, white cargo shorts, and my brown, leather Crocs (yes, there are leather Crocs). I almost regret my poor clothing decisions and then immediately shove the thought away. I'm finally actually here. Not here in a dream that I'm having while I take a nap in Algebra class. And because of this, there is no time for regrets or fears. Here, I will not be the cautious boy in Crocs who doesn't like to try new things. Here, I will be wild. Here, I will confront every fear, irrational or rational. Here, I will live. Here, I will live with no thoughts of death. Heeding to this command of my own, I run through this magnificent place and away from the airport. Away from its daunting glass façade and away from a place so full of conflicting emotions I'm surprised it (and all other airports really) hasn't imploded yet. People so full of wonder at the place they've just arrived in and people full of melancholy because they've just had to say goodbye. People happy they're back home and people crushed they now must go back home. Those people, the ones that get to call Iceland home, those are the lucky ones. The ones that get to wake up to this mysterious but incredibly alluring place and watch the sunset over this island filled with both abundances of green and places only the color white dares to inhabit. But, this is all beside the point and I already said I refused to get up in the minutia like I normally do, so I'll continue. I run, and I run, and I run, and I run, and I run and run and run. I run and my navy and white Nike sneakers snap frozen pieces of grass in two that are hidden underneath the snow. I run and my thighs start the burn because I am not a runner. But, I will have to be one today. I run until I can see the ocean. This first glimpse of the ocean happens to take place from a black, scraggly precipice. The rocks are sharp and they cut my hands in my attempt to climb to the edge. This leaves the black rocks with drop and spots of my bright red blood, glistening in the heavy sunlight. When I reach my goal of standing on the edge of this masterpiece of erosion, the wind blows and the wind blows hard. I am almost flung into the near frozen ocean, but I grab the sharp rocks behind me and I manage to not succumb to this great wind. The skin of the palms of both of my hands is torn off because of my desperate seek for an anchor, and the rocks I held onto are now more red than black. I am relieved but not satisfied because of my sudden realization that I held on because I was scared, and fear is something I have decided to let go of. So, the sacrifice of hands was for naught because I have decided I want to jump. I need to jump. I need to do the thing I was fighting so hard because of the reason I was fighting it in the first place. It's a long way down, but I walk a couple of steps back, run, and then leap into the horizon. I leap into the Sun and I leap into the ocean. I leap and I leave all of the anxiety, nerves, and worries that have been bottled up in me. I leave my past self behind and I leave the cautious boy in Crocs behind. For a second, I flying and I'm overjoyed. And then, I hit the water. I slam into the water and immediately sink. The water is as cold, dark, and empty feeling as I expect Donald Trump's heart to be and I struggle not to give up, and let my body drift lifelessly to the bottom of this unforgivable body of water. I imagine my family, and the piano, and how good it feels to play a C scale on the piano. I imagine how good it feels to dance and turn to page in a book. I imagine my life. This gives me the motivation I need to fight this water and struggle to reach the surface so I can take a breath. I do just this and as soon as my mouth is above the water and I take a giant, desperate gulp of air, a massive wave grabs me and slaps me ruthlessly against the wall of the black, scraggly precipice that I had climbed seconds before. By doing this, the wave reminds me that I will never be able to get rid of my anxiety, my nerves, or my worries, and that I will always be the cautious boy in Crocs. My last thought before entering the Clearing at the End of the Path is that at least I have died in the place I love most in the world, and that at least I know how it feels to live recklessly, even if it was only a short experiment that ended tragically.

Writing Activity

1. Write a poem or narrative about a situation where you had a chance to use your voice to speak out for someone else and you didn't. Include how you felt about your choice.

2. The author of this piece writes about youth confusing adults with their viewpoints. Write a list of some of your viewpoints on the world, your life, and culture that you feel some adults could find confusing.

3. Describe a place where you have always dreamed of going. Make sure to include colors, smells, and sounds. Write about doing something daring in that place that you would never do.

Alma Sarahi Tlachi

Alma Sarahi Tlachi was born in Puebla, Mexico. She is a junior at Santa Ana High School. Alma is the oldest of three siblings and aspires to be an example for them. Growing up, Alma has learned that life has difficult paths, however, a person is able to overcome them. "Hay que vivir un día a la vez," is a motto she lives by.

Abuse

Before She Didn't Know
What The A Word Meant
She Wildly Dance, And Lived Her Life Freely
She Still Played With her Dolls
Very Young, Very Fragile
She Found The Darkness In The World
She's Afraid To Be In Love,
Her Skin Has Been Laminated
With The Disgusting Slime,
Her Body Is Know Atrociously Scared
Even If She Scrubbed, It Doesn't Seem To Never Go Away,
She Still Sees The Ghost
And Trembles Every Night,
She Wished She Ran Away, Before She Learned What
The Word Abuse Meant.

Writing Activity

1. Alma shares a motto that she lives by. A motto is a short phrase that tries to capture the belief of a person. What is your motto? If you don't have one, create one! Create as many as you want. They can be useful to help guide you in the direction you want to go in.

2. Alma's poem explores the word 'abuse.' Write a poem where you explore the meaning of a word. Give images, feelings, and descriptions of how the word affects you.

Nomar Santana

Nomar Santana is a 17-year-old resident of Santa Ana. He lives with his mom who inspires him to always give his absolute best in everything he does. He loves his high school and the NAC because both give him a sense of community. Shadia, a tutor at the NAC, convinced Nomar to participate in the Barrio Writers program. He's glad he discovered the endless potential and power that poetry can bring even though he had no idea the program was actually going to be about poetry. He enjoys writing short films with his friends, exercising, playing piano, and for better or for worse, keeping his head in the clouds.

What I Lost and What I Gained

I lost a love for my afro
I gained a new yearn for it back
It was a part of me, an extension of myself

I lost a hate for my city
I gained a profound love for it
The people of the city gave me understanding

I lost the importance of identity
I gained the importance of embracing it
There was no joy in keeping myself in a box

I lost my sense of self hatred
I gained a sense of self love
The pursuit of positivity enabled me to make a change

Not Atlantis

I once heard of a city
Built like a bowl
Whenever it rained
Water flowed down to the center
Apparently it's the lowest point

The streets in the center collected all the water
Often they would flood
The people of the center of the city would speak up
Yet others were quick to dismiss them

They tell the people of the center:

"Tough luck it was built like that
Why don't you just swim through the streets
We can't change it
And who knows
Maybe you'll catch a fish"

Writing Activity

1. Do you not like something about yourself? Nomar wrote a poem about what society has made him not like about himself. Try it yourself. Write a poem where you explore what you don't like about yourself and why.

Adrian Michael Graham

Adrian Graham was born on January 13, 2005 in Orange, California. He is twelve years old. He lives in Downtown Santa Ana. He has a brother named Esaias. He also has three cats and a fish. He dreams of being an actor.

The Book and the Pen

This is a story
Of the Book and the Pen.
The Book was blank
and was super boring.
The Pen was full of ink
and wonderful adventures.
The Pen saw the blank
Book and had an idea.
He wrote and wrote
inside the Book.
He then sighed of exhaustion
when he finished the story that
made the Book filled with wonderful
adventures.
What happened to the Pen, you
may ask?
He died
No more ink.
Finished.
That's why I just asked
someone for a new pen.

"Identity Please."

I am a twelve-year-old boy that lives in a city filled with ghetto birds and sirens. When I'm going to school, to the store, or to my friend's house I see the marks of people dead. And because I come from Hispanic roots, people think of me as someone that doesn't belong here. I know things are changing like the life of a butterfly, but I still imagine what challenges my ancestors faced when they had to fight in wars. I fight wars too. When I go out on my bike and the police officers look at me like I just did a drug deal or killed someone. I feel like everyone is being labeled, like that man is Mexican, that kid is Canadian, that woman is Muslim. I am proud to be Mexican American and have my beliefs or to be able to think that I can be whatever I want to be when I grow up. I am proud to get out and make goals on the field. I am proud to be me. So if anyone asks me "Identity Please", this is my identity.

No Comment

You can ask me what I want to be when I grow up.
You can ask me if I love my life.
You can ask me if I like Dr. Dre or Beethoven.

But you can't make me answer the questions.
You can't make me move my mouth.
I can just stand there with a face that says, "No Comment."

People think that not answering is impolite.
Or maybe they think that I am dumb.
But sometimes I think that silence is golden.

Silence is beautiful 'cause what if I say something that will hurt.
I mean, even though I'm speaking the truth, some people aren't ready.
That's why I think silence is beautiful, like my face when it says, "No Comment."

Writing Activity

1. Society often labels groups of people with stereotypes according to age, race, class, gender, sexual orientation, physical appearance, and ability, but everyone is different and unique.

Make two lists. In the first list, write the stereotypes that society uses to label you. In the second list, write the words you use to describe yourself. What differences do you see in the two lists? Write a letter, speech, or poem about how society defines your identity and how you define yourself.

2. Think about a time when you kept quiet, but you had something to say. If you could say what you were thinking, what would you say? Write a poem about what you would have said and why you chose not to speak.

Elizabeth Whitmire

Elizabeth Whitmire is a poet and short story writer. She is currently in college and wants to move out of Texas as soon as possible. Her favorite author is the legendary Edgar Allan Poe.

Judge

The thought of sharing her words is terrorizing
She already feels every emotion intensifying
The anxiety crashes over her like a tidal wave
They will never understand how difficult times really were
But she doesn't want the silence to last
If they could read the words what would they assume?
She's weird
I can't believe she would do that
She feels too much
They see her in the light they prefer
Society refuses to accept what they don't know
No matter how low
They judge what they don't understand
She doesn't want people to judge her past
Or judge the broken pieces the ink brings out

Writing Activity

1. Fear plays an important part in everyone's life. When you come up against something you're afraid of, you have two choices: you can either run from it, or use it to inspire you. Elizabeth has a fear of speaking and sharing her writing with other people. However, she used this piece to inspire her to conquer that fear. Look inside of yourself, and write down some of your biggest fears. What does this fear do to you? How does it make you feel? Now, write a piece about conquering that fear. Use your voice, your words, as your weapon.

Olivia Goodley

Olivia Goodley was born and raised in Houston Texas. They love corgis and wants to live in New York with 5 corgis. Their biggest dreams are to be a therapist, writer, and activist.

Oppression

"I didn't listen to the parental advisory warning on American Idiot and now
I'm gay and I hate the government"
-generationnothin

Oppression is like being a goldfish
in a bowl too small.
The owner thinks you're content
living a perfect life.
Don't pay no mind
they're just fine.
The goldfish is
stuck
trapped
cramped
It needs a larger tank
it deserves a larger tank to live its life
The owner doesn't notice
or care for that matter
"Why should I get a larger tank
it's doing just fine in a fishbowl?
It's not like it matters"
That's when the fish starts fighting
trying to free itself
jump
flail
Do whatever you can
When it finally gets out of its confines
There's nothing
No water to land in
Nothing but air
"Oh my fish died, there's always more"
The fish keep jumping
Splashing
Making a mess

Getting attention
The owner keeps buying
"It's too much of a hassle to give them a tank"
Something has to change
We splash
And we jump
Until we get our rights
We riot
We protest
We boycott buses
And we throw bricks
We don't rest
Till we get what is ours
Our basic rights
Are not decided by our oppressors
you label us as criminals
Predators
drug lords
We do not live to exist in your fishbowl

Writing Activity

1. What is oppression to you? Write a poem where you explore oppression through metaphors. What is oppression like? What would you compare it to?

2. Olivia uses an epigraph, a short quote, saying, lyric, etc. that begins a poem or story. What are some quotes that have inspired you? Write a poem inspired by that quote.

Jasmine C. Bell

Jasmine C. Bell is 20 years old, a poet, and artist in Austin, Texas. She currently attends the University of Texas with plans to major in Psychology and minor in Mandarin Chinese. She was a member of the UT Spitshine slam poetry team that went to CUPSI from 2015-2017, and will co-coach the 2018 team. In 2016, Jasmine also competed in Rustbelt 2016. She is Co-President of the only poetry organization on UT's campus (Spitshine Poetry) where she leads workshops and organizes open mics. She has authored one chapbook ("The Tears of Genesis"), has her poetry published or forthcoming in Monstering Magazine and Apricity Magazine, and drew the cover of Rattle's Magazine's "Tribute to Poets with Mental Illness." She loves Studio Ghibli and Steven Universe and spends her time writing, studying, drawing, singing, and eating.

Portrait of the Woman as a New Planet (feat. Trauma)

I was once gravity.
I collected every rock and ember
to build my sphere.
I let the rolling landscape of my body
boil over with lava and steam.

I was a new world:
scorching and ready for all the universe.
I engulfed every rock though it scarred my surface,
though it twisted my crust into an unnamed shape.

Passing asteroids whispered cautionary tales.
I tell myself that this only happens in other star systems;
Jupiter will protect me, sling any intruder
right back into the endlessness of space.

One day, a man says he wants to touch me,
run his bouldered hands all over.
I say no,
so he throws a rock the size of a war god.

Pieces of me are everywhere.
Dirt encircles me and I can't keep track
of all the bits.

Over time, the scattered shards coalesce.
trauma becomes a life-long companion
and I name her moon.

She never leaves.
But sometimes, she reflects light,
reminds me that I am capable of surviving,
of harboring life,
of being my own home.

Writing Activity

1. If you were a planet, which would you be and why? How do your characteristics and life experiences connect to a planet's?

2. How do our life experiences shape us? Write about a moment in your life that shaped you and made you the person you are today.

3. If you feel able, write a story about a painful life experience. This can be truth or fiction. How did you or the main character cope with that experience? As this writer did, you may choose to write in the voice of another character (this is called a persona).

Alexis Williams

Alexis was born in Nacogdoches, Texas on the second day of December. Her mother was always a working woman and didn't have enough money growing up, so she lived with her grandmother for a while. She'd move in and out of town every so often because of her mother going back into the military again. She made a handful of friends from different schools every time she got the chance to. lexis never liked school that much but one thing she did like was language arts class. She could write her tail off. Her work didn't have to be good. She'd write about everything that was going on. It was the only time she could express what she was feeling.

The Right Path

She was lost and confused in a sea full of people. She didn't know where to go and never knew where to turn. She was always so confused on where was where, which way was which, and who was who. But then came along a nice young boy who took her under his wing. He was kind and always had a smile on his face. His bone structure was perfect. Buff and all. Once they got to know each other, she told him about being lost. He looked at her with his dark brown eyes and smiled. Glad he was going to show her the way. She thought he was the greatest. He was actually showing her something that she was longing for. She looked at him with grateful eyes and thanked him. Since then, they've had a wonderful relationship. She was glad to have someone like this in her life. "Could it be love?", she thought. Because in her eyes, he truly did care. She wanted him to stay with her forever.

One day, the boy said he was going to find another path. The girl was excited. She wanted to go, too. The boy told her to stay, as it was important that he'd go alone. It didn't make since to her. They've gone everywhere together and now he wants her to stay? She was hesitant at first, but then let him go. It was important, right? He went. She waited on him for 5 days and 5 nights until realizing he abandoned her. He wasn't coming back. She didn't understand. She thought he loved her. Why would he lie to her and leave so suddenly?

Now, she was all alone again. In the sea full of bodies. Lost and confused. She was starting to think that he was showing her the wrong path. But at the same time, she didn't think anyone could take his place. But if someone did come along would they show her the right path?

Writing Activity

1. Alexis shares in her bio that her path often moved in and out of towns due to her mom's military service. The character in her short story "The Right Path" talks about having many paths, too, and appears to be so comforted when she finds someone willing to share a path with her. In the end, the character believes that the path was the "wrong path," after all. Take some time to think about a path you have followed that turned out to be the wrong one, a path you wish you had taken and have always imagined what would have happened if you had, a path that you decided to stray from, or a path you are currently on. Now, write a narrative "map" about one of those paths that leads your readers through the choices that got you on/off the path, who did/didn't join you on your path, where your path went/didn't go, etc.

2. In her bio, Alexis claims, "She could write her tail off. Her work didn't have to be good. She'd write about everything that was going on. It was the only time she could express what she was feeling." Embrace Alexis' free-to-be-her writing style and just write… about ANYTHING and EVERYTHING. And don't stop! Good writers write everyday… they write something, anything, everything. Start a habit of writing… and don't stop!

Noble Peck

Noble is 13 years old with a track record of the comedic variety. He lives to write in a casual style and enjoys reading science fiction. He was born in 2003 in San Antonio, Texas weighing only two pounds. Noble aspires to go to NYU and to be on the comedy show Saturday Night Live.

Color

Golden birds circle a green tree
Leaves fall onto perfect green grass
Red buds poke from within the leaves, willing their voices to be heard
A black raven stands on a branch searching for a white mouse scurrying through the grass
Lazy golden yellow fish float aimlessly in a reflective pool
No trash in sight
This is before we came
Soon brown brick smokestacks will turn the sky black with smoke
Golden birds will fall to the earth like stones unable to breathe in the polluted air
The tree will have been chopped down to make wood for the fires
The buds will wilt and die because the rain is acid and the smog covers the sun
The raven will have starved because the mice will have died from lack of plants to eat
The golden yellow fish will choke on trash and other waste that now fills their pond
This is what we we're doing to our home
Some of you may ask how we are doing this
The real question is how will we stop it.

Writing Activity

1. In the poem, the author uses colors to describe the landscape before "we" come to the land. Think about what "we" look like. Does the "we" have a color? What color(s)? Write a description of the "we."

2. Write a response in any form (poem, prose, etc.) to answer the question, "How will we stop it?" Use colors and imagery to answer the questions.

Gracie O'Dell

Gracie O'Dell was born in Spartanburg, South Carolina and later moved to Garrison, Texas at the age of three. Growing up with two brothers, she would spend time watching Disney movies, YouTube videos, and Netflix, listening to various types of music, and reading books. She has participated in band, Model United Nations, and UIL competitions. She will be attending Nacogdoches High School as a freshman in the fall of 2017. When Gracie is older, she would like to work as a SFX makeup artist in live theater and movie production, with dreams of writing books mainly directed at teens and young adults.

Evangeline's Choice

I wipe the sweat from my forehead, my pale, ghost-like skin glistening in the soft pink light coming from the lanterns illuminating the bathroom. I try to brush my long, pink hair back as I splash my face with water. The dreams have happened again. The ones where evil consumes all and light refuses to shine. Even in my dreams, I do not know what side I'm on.

"Another nightmare?" a familiar voice asks as I dry off my face with a fluffy blue towel.

"Not now," I reply, slightly annoyed.

"I just want to help," the voice pushes further, "you need to see your mother, she can help." I turn to face her, knowing she was right. She always was.

"I know," I sigh, "I wish my fairy godmother wasn't so right all the time."

"That's my job, sweetheart." She tells me. I roll my eyes. Yes, giving your godchild advice was part of being a fairy godmother, along with other things, but being right was not in the job description.

"Don't call me that, Petunia," I say, knowing how much her own name annoys her. Petunia and I never really got along. When my father died, the Court of Fairies decided it was necessary to give me a fairy godmother, so they assigned me Petunia. At first it was okay, but ten years of constantly being followed and scolded by a flying sparkle machine, or having to constantly follow and scold a prissy princess, gets to you.

"Are you always going to call me that?" She asks me, pouting, "What if I wanted to be called Muffin instead?" I cough, trying to keep myself from laughing. The name would make a lot of sense, considering her figure was the shape of a muffin, but I wasn't about to tell her that.

"There's no way I'm calling you that, Petunia." I say as I walk from the bathroom into the long, dark hallway.

"Well, good luck with your mother, Evangeline." She tells me, before disappearing into a cloud of shimmers.

I enter the Great Hall, where my mother sits on her behemoth stone throne, dramatic as always. When she sees me, she seems to perk up a little, but then returns to her cold, stern, facial expression. She stands up and gestures, "Evangeline, come with me to the window," she says, "having the dreams again? That means you're ready to join me." I walk with her to the window, where her own pale, blue-tinted skin seems blinding in the sunlight, and her black hair shifts into blues and greens like crow feathers, much different than the bubblegum hue of my own hair. I look out onto the hill, where the bloody battle is taking place. "You see those brave citizens fighting? All creatures want to end this battle for good, and stop my evil sister from taking over the land." My mother speaks as if she's talking to a possible ally, which I guess I am now. As she speaks, I look out over the bright, green grass, now covered in the different colored blood of fairies, nymphs, centaurs, and witches. I don't blame them for wanting to end the war. It's been going on since I was a small child, and I have never known true peace myself.

I think about my aunt. I don't know much about her, but from what little I remember, she looked like me, with a sharp face and pink hair, and she definitely never seemed evil. Then I begin to wonder what even started the war. My whole life I had been told by my mother and royal advisors that it was because my aunt wanted to subdue the land with her dark magic. Despite this, Petunia had told me that my mother and aunt had arguments that were more complicated, and that magic could never be truly good or evil. And since fairies cannot lie, I believed her.

"So," my mother's voice breaks me from my trance, "are you ready to join me, Evangeline?" I stand there for a moment, still looking at the gory scene outside the window. Knowing I have to make a decision, I nod. My mother smiles "You made the right choice." I can tell that she's never been prouder. I continue to look out towards the battlefield, and as I witness all the bloodiness, all the death and horror, I begin to wonder, Who is good? And who is evil?

Writing Activity

1. As children, we believe that what our parents and adults tell us is completely true. However, as we get older, we realize that some situations are never black/white or right/wrong. The more experiences and education we have, the way we think and see situations changes. Write about something you believed as a child but now question as a young adult.

2. Try writing a fairy tale. Imagine that you are having a nightmare and you wake up to find a fairy godmother visiting you. What does she/she say? Do you learn anything from the encounter?

Isis Rivera

Isis Rivera is 12 years old, and she's from Austin, Texas. She enjoys writing as a great stress reliever and to express her feelings. She writes in a diary type way, in seriousness to help her take some stress off her plate. She enjoys being athletic. She has been a part of soccer, softball, volleyball, shot put and dance. She has won national championships in softball and many school writing competitions. She wishes to go to St. Edward's University.

Well Hasn't Everybody

I am a young lady
I am a Puerto Rican Latina
I am bold, sassy, outgoing yet shy at certain points, I'm bossy but friendly, and a sometimes confident young lady

Although I am all of that, I am also judged
Well isn't everybody
I'm not the thinnest person
I'm not the prettiest girl
I'm not the most popular
I'm not the most liked
I'm not the richest person
My ethnicity is different than others too

Yet I understand I'm different
I accept that I'm different in my own way, I guess
I have my insecurities but I know I'm special

Well isn't everybody special
But for me it's different
When people judge me, it crawls under my skin
I know then that I'm not special
I tell myself that I can't change
I'm the same ugly, fat, unpopular girl that everyone knows I am

I feel unwanted, useless, uncared for
I feel pain and heart break
Well hasn't everybody felt like this before
I feel the same way I've felt all my life, just a person with no meaning
I want to stop feeling like this

The world is cruel
The people in it are evil
What the people say is hurtful
When they bring the words to action it's painful

I can be strong but not everyone can stay strong forever
It all one day will push me past my limit, when I can't take it anymore
I've been through a lot
Well hasn't everybody
I man yea, but I'm not that strong and hopeful
I know I'll be pushed to my breaking point
I know I'm not special
I know I'm different
I know I'm not the way I should be

That's just me
The one who can't be the way everyone wants her to be
The one who shuts herself down
The one who is left
The one who is depressed, sad, in pain
The one person I wish I didn't have to be
Well doesn't everyone feel like that sometimes

Writing Activity

1. Isis uses the line "Well doesn't everyone/Well hasn't everybody" as repetition to drive a specific point home. Repetition is a literary technique used for emphasis and rhythmic effect. Write something (a short story, poem, even a song) that employs repetition throughout the piece.

2. Think about a time you have felt "not special" and "not the way [you] should be." Who or what made you feel that way? How did you deal with this feeling?

3. In the beginning of this piece, Isis balanced multiple identities with her negative feelings—bold, sassy, outgoing and shy, friendly, and confident. The rest of the poem reads like a confessional. Think of something that's always bothered you, and someone you're comfortable confessing to. Write a letter to them about the thing that is bothering you.

Minh Ly

Minh Ly was born in Vietnam on May 9, 2002. He came to the United States in 2012. He started learning English and made new friends, and now some of them have become his best friends. He goes to Valley High School, and he's in his sophomore year. He joined the Anteater Academy and Nicholas Academic Center to help him go to college.

Life

People's lives are just like a blank paper
Some people get to fill it
While others don't
Because part of the paper was already filled in
So you have to erase it and fill it back in
But there is people that just fill it in without erasing
Everyone gets to choose what they want to do

Writing Activity

1. Minh uses a simile, a comparison of one thing to another using 'like' or 'as,' to compare a person's life to a sheet of paper. Give it a try. Compare a life to an object in a poem using the template: "People's lives are like _____." What do you discover about life?

Robert Andaluz

Robert Andaluz was born on December 20th 2002, Santa Ana, California. He grew up with his parents living at his mom's mother's house and then moved out to a quieter and calmer neighborhood. There he met new friends and people. His hobbies are hanging out with friends, watching YouTube, and eating. He became a Barrio Writer because his mother is obsessed with his education and thought he needed to improve his writing skills. He is currently a freshman at Godinez Fundamental High school and is a part of their football team.

I Am

I Hate You, I Hate You, And I Hate You. You bring me down when I and try to stand up. You make me less interesting than I really am. You lower my confidence when I need it the most. You make me feel isolated when there are millions of people around me. I am confident without you. I am funny without you. I am talkative without you. I am interesting without you. When I do something new, you are always with me. I wish you were gone so I could be who I really am. Someday…Someday I will overcome you.

Writing Activity

1. Many consider 'hate' to be a powerful word. What do you 'hate?' Write a poem dedicated to what you hate and how you will overcome it. It can be useful to explore difficult and powerful feelings through art.

Adrian Gutierrez

My name is Adrian Gutierrez, born June 9, 2005. I have one brother and one sister. I am the middle child, and it has not been difficult because my older brother does most of the chores at home. My favorite leisure is to play soccer. Soccer is my strongest sport but I would also love to play basketball. Even though I get my ankles broken by my older brother, my shot is way better than his. Also, why I like to be the middle child is because now I am teaching my sister how to play soccer. Now comes the difficult part of my life, middle school. School isn't my strongest point but I would like to keep improving in certain subjects, especially reading. I will like to play soccer in school so I really need to improve.

Happiness

Happy I am
Happy I be
With all the wonders of sports
Soccer is the Best
Strong as can be
Skillful as I try
Failure is Not Best!

Writing Activity

1. What is your favorite sport? Write a piece where you explore your favorite sport. What are the rules? How do you play it? What does the sport say about your life?

Pedro Flores

Pedro Flores was born in Santa Ana. He was raised by both his mom and dad. When he turned 3, he went to preschool for only 3 days and his grandparents took him out. He turned 5 and went to kindergarten, but he noticed that he was a little bit bigger. He then turned 6 and went to 1st grade. The year ended and he was told that he flunked. His parents were mad at him so his mom moved him to Tustin and he was in school till 3rd grade. He then went to a program called CDC. After that, he moved back to Santa Ana in the 4th grade. He was always the bigger kid, but he didn't care because his father always told him that people called him names but he didn't care. After he heard that, he didn't care what people said to him. Well, he did listen to his teachers and parents as well as his older brother…you get the point. He went to fifth grade, and he fell in love with a girl but never had the guts to ask her to be his girlfriend. He graduated so his older brother told him about Barrio Writers but he already knew because he always went to his performances. He joined Barrio Writers this year.

Who am I

What color am I
What race am I
What do I stand out for.
What do I do. What's my
Culture. What's my color.
I am tan.
My hair is purple.
I have differences.
I am gay.
I am happy.
Who am I.

Painting

The white wave of lines that glow into the
blue background. You kind of hear the waves. You
imagine the Zzzzzing from the snakes of the white lines.
The painting takes me to a place like cartoons.
I got into another painting of the car that was on fire.
It makes me imagine an enemy bursting into Flames and trying to say,
Sorry! I'm sorry about what I did to you!

I could not stand him bursting to tears for his forgiveness.
I loved to see him suffer but I had to stop. I felt bad for him.
I took him out of the car but he was facing downwards so
I turned him upwards.
I saw his face and
It was me.

My Latino Street

My Latino Street is amazing! I hear gun shots but I'm watching the T.V at home. I have a secret room. You want to know why it's a secret?
I love the red smelly house. I love that the house is a bright red. It lets the firefighters know that we live here.
I hate the smell! It smells like blood. The blood of bodies; the blood from the innocent people.
Our house never gets shot at because we glow. We have differences from our Latino Street.

Writing Activity

1. In "Who am I," Pedro explores identity by first presenting questions about himself and then responding with his own answers. Make a list of the questions others have asked you or that you have asked yourself. Write a poem in which you respond to those questions.

2. "Painting" is an ekphrastic poem inspired by Lucio Muniain's "Are You Skeptical?" exhibition.

An ekphrastic poem is a dramatic description of a work of art. Ekphrastic poets describe drawings, paintings, sculptures, or life scenes. Ekphrastic descriptions can be realistic or imaginary.

Try writing an ekphrastic poem. Look at a drawing, painting, sculpture, photograph, or just look in front of you and start describing what you see. Describe how the art or scene engages your senses and what it makes you think of.

3. Think about your street, neighborhood, or house. Make a list of the things you like about it. Then make a list about what you think it needs. Write a poem describing your street, neighborhood or house. Think about the sights, sounds, smells, and other sensations you experience.

Logun Claeys

Logun Claeys is from Corpus Christi, TX with hopes of attending Texas A&M University - Corpus Christi. He enjoys robots and taking machines apart to discover their inner-workings. Although he writes in all genres, he most enjoys writing short stories.

My Weekly Summary

Being at the Barrio Writers workshop this past week was fun. Before it began I thought it was going to be boring, but being able to write my own stories is nice. I would like to give credit to Robin, Carmen, and Cameron for teaching me new forms of writing. One of my favorite things about this week was our field trip to the art museum. I liked how some art had a story to it while some art was funny to look at. So this is my story.

Writing Activity

1. When thinking about perspective, it's important to remember that we all live different lives. We think about and experience things in different ways. Write a summary of your week, and how it made you feel. What did you like about it? What didn't you like about it? Who experience these things with you?

Courtney Michelle Roberts

Courtney Michelle Roberts is a 13-year-old activist and entrepreneur. At just the tender age of 11, Courtney created her Instagram blog "Everydayblackgirl." She uses her platform to tackle and talk about issues such as Intersectional Feminism, Black Empowerment, and LGBTQ rights with all 63.8k of her followers. Not only does she own such an amazing page, she also owns her own business, titled "Everydayblackgirl," where she will begin marketing social and political themed t-shirts/merchandise this upcoming summer.

The Box

The box. The box you created. The box they created.
When I say they, I mean the people who make you think the way you do.
They are the reason I wrote this poem.
This poem is about me. When I say me, I mean us.
When I say us, I mean the people you don't recognize.
The people you overlooked.
The people you threw into that box.
The box you created.
The box they created.

Writing Activity

1. Write about a time you experienced someone having expectations for you that you did not want or agree to? Describe your feelings in a poem, narrative, song, rap, or graphic.

2. Do you have expectations of other people's behavior? What are those expectations? Have you spoken them, or are they just something you expect? Write about a time when someone didn't meet your expectations, and how you felt in that situation.

Cesar Villanueva

ReColt Villanueva was born on February 1, 2002. He is the oldest of two siblings. He has a family of five, which consists of parents and two sisters. ReColt likes school and loves to play videogames. He is really good at survival games and enjoys learning new things. ReColt is a sophomore at Santa Ana Valley High school as of 2017. He wants to go to college and become a Computer Hardware Engineer. For fun, ReColt likes to take electronics apart and see how things work. ReColt enjoys school and when he has free time, he goes to work to save for college. ReColt dreams of owning real estate and make it his profession.

Loss

Loss is a terrible thing to happen
Why do we lose the ability to say hi to family members?
Lost memories are hard to recover
Losing privileges can be a pain
The loss of a family member is unbearable
Do we really need to lose, to win?

Through loss, new understandings are obtained
Failure gains you supportive friends when you lose family
Responsibility and respect are gained through loss
I have gained eyes that can see the good in people
Through losing, knowledge and skills have been gained
Through losing memories, you recreate them, and gain independence through mistakes
Losing is the key to winning.

Writing Activity

1. When have you lost something? How did you feel? What did you learn from the experience? Write a poem where you explore what loss can teach you.

Alexis Avila

Alexis Avila is a senior in the Health Science Academy. He has three passions and writing happens to be one. He is the eldest of two siblings, and he also loves his mom. With her helpful pushing, Alexis has decided to pursue a degree in nursing.

Drought

She lives with the moon standing on contorted trees not lurking but searching
Calling to the ground in hopes of answers
But even his worn vegetation suffers, no flowers bear fruit
In desperate times she recklessly destroys life in hopes that
Mother Earth will send her sweet serenity to wash the sins of the world.

Oxytocin

Get your dose of Oxytocin
3:31am on your roof exchanging
Ideas of what our celestial bodies would say if we were together
Get your dose of Oxytocin
But we both knew the consequence,
That we'd only create smoke, smoke that will aid the vivid image I have of you
I overdosed on Oxytocin
You never could withstand my heat
Full moons illuminate what we'd rather keep in the dark
Don't worry it isn't your fault
I overdosed on Oxytocin

The time we lost

My youth is like trying to touch the horizon
Wanting to feel where heaven meets earth
Constantly chasing to have that satisfaction
To have my hands on the impossible
So I chase
My bare face can still feel the warm sun on my cheeks
So I chase
My running turns to sprinting, this however makes me sweat,
My heart beats faster my legs are working

So I chase
Still relying on my youth to carry me, the warmth grows and my hand wipes my face that is no longer bare
Signs of aging begin to appear
So I chase
Fatigue begins to challenge my youth the sun begins to set
So I chase
It's been some time now the sun has set
I see my reflection my youth has faded, the moon has risen
And I never got to touch the horizon

Writing Activity

1. Alexis' poem Ocytocin is inspired by a natural chemical in the brain that initiates bonding and love. Write a poem about something or someone that you love. Describe why you love it/them and include a specific memory you have with that person/item.

2. In poetry, repetition is used to emphasize a point the speaker is making. Write a poem where you repeat a phrase, chant, or word in order to emphasize an idea to your audience.

Ricardo Morales Perez

Hey, let me tell you about my myself. I was born in Chihuahua, México on October 18, 1999 at 1:25 p.m. Being the youngest and fifth member in the family, it was nice and simple back then. But it all started when I was diagnosed with glaucoma, and then that changed me who I am today. We had to go the United States to help me to not get my condition worse and worse, but I know it is not going to stop who I am going to be the future as an activist and radio personality.

An atheist boy living with a catholic family.

What I have to say I'm not that much of a believer I'm more of a free spirit person, free thinker, helper and a man of science what I'm saying is I don't think god doesn't exist. But I want to tell you how hard it is living with my catholic family as an atheist it all started maybe around March or February I want to tell to tell my family that I was a non – believer but I was scared what they see in me like as a good person or bad one but I told all my friends in Instagram that I was a non - believer most of them respected me who I am and most of them hated me that I was an atheist but later on I promise myself I will tell my family but I forgot my sister was following me on Instagram and she figure out early on so one time we visit her and she said " are you really joking being an atheist or are you being serious". So I had think quick because it was too soon to tell them and I said to her "no Julie I'm joking that's it." I knew that was a close one I knew I would be fucked if my parent's found out early. On the next the day me and my parents stayed with my sister place so they were getting for church and I still was sleep and by the time I woke up I had a huge headache and my stomach was hurting so much. So I told my parents I wasn't feeling that good so stayed just play games, watch videos and hearing music on my phone and then time pass and my mom came from church she saw me with anger in her eyes with flames she said why I became an atheist and she explain why being an atheist is wrong but I know what she is saying is bullshit coming from her mouth that she said they rob, kill, do drugs and I swear so much bullshit she saying is stupid I don't kill people and sometimes I do rob a candy bar once while and I never do drugs but I might smoke medical weed for only glaucoma eye. But when my mom saying all that stuff she said about me is like I'm left alone the world and that no one wants to be around me. As a couple of days past by I was still thinking what my mom what saying about me and it was driving me crazy but always remember this quote about being myself and it goes. "Being confident is the key to life. Don't be afraid to be you!" I'm super different from a lot kid my age with style and personality and I'm ok with it and if you're ok everyone else will be, too just be yourself. When I always hear that in my mind I think to myself we are all different in our way like in style, personality and living life and just being us in our own different way and how we act.

Hispanic boy Living in a Stereotype Nation

I've been called a drug dealer one time at my old school
I don't know who but didn't care
But I know it was inaccurate what he thinks about me because I'm not that type of person

I'm the type of person who works hard for their money
Not selling crack, meth, heroin, or any kind of drugs
I'm the type of person who gets what he needs by working hard for it and that's it

But just the color of my skin and my race doesn't mean I sell drugs
But I didn't give a rat's ass. I'm a human being
Who is trying to live life as a Hispanic immigrant.

Build That Wall

I always hear those three words
Build.That.Wall
It funny how some trump voters think trump is going make American Great Again
but there is one way that Donald Trump can make American great Again and it is that he should
Quit
Because what I see in the wall
Yes it could keep some bad people away
but what about the good people
trying to live a better life
trying to escape the violence, death, gangs and the drugs
and trying to help their children to have a better future
to someone great like a ceos, doctors, scientists, business people, teachers, soldiers
So trump when hear this
Make sure take out your brain
Make sure it doesn't have any dust or garbage
Because it's so stupid
What you thinking?

Writing Activity

1. Write a poem, song, rap, or narrative about your view of your family's religious or nonreligious beliefs. How has this shaped you, and what would your experience be if you decided that your beliefs were different from your family's viewpoints?

2. Write about a time when someone found out that you believe something different from them, and how did they respond? Did they still pursue a friendship with you or did they choose to not be friends anymore? Why do you think people make these types of decisions based on what others believe?

3. Write about some cultural stereotypes about you that are not true. Why is it important that people see past cultural stereotypes and discover your unique individuality?

4. What are some issues in your community, state, or nation that you do not agree with? Why do you not agree? How can you use your voice to have influence with people that make these types of decisions?

5. Why is it important for youth to use their voice to help shape the culture, actions, and laws of their country? What is something that you can be involved in at home, at school, or in your community to make it a better place for all people that live there?

Taylor Gates

I'm Taylor. I'm the youngest of three kids. I have a brother and a sister. I come from a very athletic family. We love watching and playing sports and we are very competitive with each other.

My Own Race

Once upon a time there was this little girl her mom was mixed with Asian and Mexican her dad was mixed with White and Black and every day she would wonder what race am I. I'm not fully Black. I'm not fully White. I'm not full Mexican. I'm not fully Asian. What am I, she always wondered thought out her life thought elementary, middle school, and high school she'd asked herself that question every day. When she got into college she got her first boyfriend and he knew what she was going through, because he was going through the same thing he was. His parents were mixed to his mom was mixed with Easter Egypt and Canadian and his dad was mixed with Russian and Native American. He told her that she was special and probably the first of her race and that is how you should look at things. Now she sees things from a different perspective she see herself as her own race and she's proud of it.

Writing Activity

1. For many, how we identify can help to define who we are to ourselves as well as to others. However, for many of us, we are not solely one thing as the speaker in this piece has stated. Make a list of the different aspects that make up your identity. Think about these facets; do they conflict? How are they different from how others see you?

2. How could the speaker's racial ambiguity be difficult for her to function and move through our society? Is it easier to pick a race, gender, orientation, etc., or to become your own special identity? Write about what it would be like to declare yourself as a new and unique race from others. What cultural tradition, language, religion, dress, etc., would you have? How would others react?

David Kotkin

My name is David Kotkin. I am 18 years old and attend Beckman High School. My hobbies are Historical Studies and Politics. I am a part of Junior Senators of America, a club that has members around the United States where people debate legislation and even make their own. I have created and passed a bill for the Veteran Affairs (VA) which increased the responsibilities and budget of the VA. I am also a part of Big Brothers Big Sisters of Orange County where I tutor children who otherwise could not afford one. I hope to become an educator or a politician so I can aid those who otherwise would not be helped.

Want To Make A Deal?

To some eyes I am good, protective, and nice,
But when the lights go out and the Bibles come out,
I strike like El Diablo,
Attacking your soul and pride,
And as you lose your will to live,
I begin to drill under your feet and force you to leave what you thought of as paradise,
As you fall you lose all sense of love and wake up in your new hellish afterlife,
Falling to your knees you begin to plead,
Seeing the fear in your eyes,
I offer you my wicked price,
For your safe return to paradise,
Accepting my devilish price,
You begin to leave as I look at my new deed,
Smiling at the deal you and I have agreed.

Writing Activity

1. What sort of deal is made in David's poem? Why would the speaker be happy to make this deal? Is the poem from the perspective of a villain? Give it a try. Write from the point of view from a villainous figure. What do you think they'll focus on? What do you think they want?

Anonymous

I'm a girl that is not very good at writing. I am a participant in the Houston Barrio Writers 2017 program.

Happiness

The sun's up and glistening on the concrete just like the day before, some days brighter than ever but I'm glad I even get to see the day's light
Around my room, I'm alone but not so alone in city with 8 million people and along with my cat
I go outside and see so many new faces every day and happy I'm a part of them
Days here don't seem to ever get boring in this city that never sleeps

Writing Activity

1. This poet chose to remain anonymous, someone who chooses to not be identified. Why do you think that is? What freedom do you get when you can write without an identity? What are the limitations? What would you say if you were anonymous. Write something with the intention of remaining anonymous.

Taylor Nicole Williams

Taylor Nicole Williams is a 16-year-old teenager born and raised in Round Rock Texas. She is a member of her school's student council as well as a member of the Round Rock Library Teen Council. Her hobbies include reading as many books as she can find and going on adventures with her dog.

The Holding of a Heart

If my heart was to be held
Then my feelings would be humbly felt
If they are frosted in ice during winter
Come Spring they would melt

I come with the breeze of warming nights
Laid to bed by those held close
Keeping the demons inside
To not touch those she loved most

While a thorn may fall of be laid?
On my prized oak chair
With a poisoned crown on top of my head
I will be brave enough to dare

I will not fall to my feet and quake
And for your sake
You should know I have no problem laying waste
I have the right to give myself just as much so as take

Writing Activity

1. In her poem, Taylor uses rhymes at the end of her lines and four-line stanzas to create rhythm. Choose a poem you've written that is more free-form, and experiment with how you can use structures like this to create rhythm.

2. How has the poet used images like "poisoned crown" and "frosted fingers" to discuss a relationship between the speaker and someone else? What is the effect?

3. Write a poem about a relationship (friendly, familial or romantic) that uses uncommon images to convey the relationship you have or seek. What would those images be?

Samantha Sanchez

My name is Samantha (Sam, Sammii). I am 16 years old (I wish I was 17 already so I can buy rated R movie tickets by myself). I attend Fountain Valley High School (which is actually pretty great not going to lie) and in the fall, I will be a junior. I adore living in California (but after high school I'd love to be somewhere that actually has a real winter). I am a fourth-generation woman Gemini (I do not have a twin).

I am heavily involved in my schools track and field program (physically and mentally difficult but rewarding). This will be my first year in Link Crew (I'm excited). I also hope to be on Senate this year and eventually I hope to be on ASB (by the end of junior year). I am interning at Grand Central Art Center (which I hope to make into a job) because of Girls Inc. (I have been a strong, smart, and bold woman since the summer of 7th grade)

Wherever I may end up in the future, I hope I am happy with who I am and what I am doing (truly).

Two Faced

Elements of air, light green and yellow
The strength of affection, curiosity and adaptability
Expressive and quick-witted
But indecisive, nervous, and inconsistent
Two personalities rolled up into one
But fascinated with every inch of the world

Uncertainty

Imagine
A white, creamy, sandy beach
In the middle of June
Her smile is pure sunlight
That we don't even need the beaming sun anymore
The waves are fierce and chaotic yet calming
As they mellow out and crash to the shore
She is mesmerized by the beauty of turquoise, whites, and bubbles
That she does not realize the immensity of it all
The dangers and uncertainty of being sucked in by the dark matter
We do not know what dark matter is

Questions About this Life

The following questions are asked by a curious mind and the answers are answered by open minds. There are many stereotypes, labels and/or standards that we place on not only others but on ourselves. This piece is about asking a variety of societal questions to see how real teens around the Huntington Beach area would respond to them. For privacy reasons each individual answer will be left anonymous. Thank you to those who were and weren't willing to open their minds and share their raw experiences with me, the curious mind.

1. How high are social standards?

Anonymous #1:

"I believe social standards are very high and take a toll on a person's life whether they like to believe it or not. Due to living near the beach (specifically Huntington Beach), there is an instant pressure of looking a certain way despite a specific gender. There's this automatic standard of the "beach babe" or "hot surfer dude" that I know and many other people that feel the need to look up to. Not to mention, being the one that goes out every night living it up at parties and doing things you know you shouldn't do but do them anyway."

2. What is one of the biggest social pressures that you feel has impacted you the most?

Anonymous #2:

"The biggest social pressure that's impacted me the most would probably be feeling the need to always have to do sexual things with guys in order to keep them close. Once I got into high school that's when it hit me the most. I got in the mindset that in order to make a guy happy I had to do sexual things with them. I thought that if I didn't give them what they wanted, they would leave me. I never understood my worth. I didn't need to be giving up myself for guys just so I could feel like I was something special to them. I feel like I wanted attention so badly from a guy I was willing to do whatever it took. I wanted to be loved by someone so much and I thought that was the only way I could win them over. Of course, it only worked if I kept doing what they wanted. It wasn't until 2 years later I finally realized I was in the wrong mindset the whole time. I took time and had a reality check. I told myself this wasn't the way—this wasn't how I was going to find love. I needed to take time and learn how to love myself before I tried to love anyone else. I finally found my worth."

Anonymous #3:

"New experiences are my shit. I am so down to try new things. I mean of course, I feel this pressure and nasty feeling in my stomach but it's always worth it after.

I knew a boy from school, close in my friend group but nothing more, nothing less. We became friends the week of my 16th birthday and let me tell you I wasn't uncomfortable when I was near him. He made me feel present and not wonder what was going on later. Long story short, I am now dating him and getting into the relationship and keeping it going has been hard on me. I wouldn't say I'm scared but I wouldn't say I'm not fearful either. I feel pressure every day, ever since the beginning of the relationship. This was a different kind of relationship than what I was used to. Bonds with family and friends were the relationships I was used to. Getting into this, came with different opinions and needs from people that I didn't need opinions from. They still had an impact on me though. I have grown to push away the opinions of others that are inconvenient but take into consideration the ones that don't know how to correctly word their help."

3. What is your interpretation of love at this age in this community?

Anonymous #4:

"I've always struggled to find what the actual meaning of love is, and I think that I've always complicated it when it's definition is different amongst all people. My interpretation of love is seeing someone for who they truly are, with all their flaws and insecurities and finding a way to accept, support, and stay with them emotionally no matter the circumstances. I also feel that when you love somebody you're willing to put them before yourself in almost all aspects."

4. How has your style or personality evolved from the people you've surrounded yourself with?

Anonymous #5:

"You know, the people I have surrounded myself with have influenced me into things that I do regret. Recently, very recently actually, I've discovered who I am as person. I'm maturing and seeing what friends have been great friends all along and have been there for me. Now I'm realizing who isn't really there and has never ever been. I'm really starting to notice who's real in my life. It's definitely a time in my life right now where I'm progressing to be a better person to and for myself and staying true to others. Being around so many people that are negative on the inside and don't care for others or themselves, is what has really affected me 100%. I do want to say that I am so incredibly thankful of most of my friends that have come into my life. I don't even know where I'd be without so many important people. So many memories have been made in my life that a lot of teenage boys don't get to have and that's thanks to the amazing friends I have. These certain friends have built me into the person I am today."

Anonymous #6:

"Growing up I've always been an extremely sentimental and emotional person. In middle school I think I was pretty confident and had a lot of friends which fed into that but as I entered high school, my circle got smaller and I soon learned who actually cared for me. After many ended relationships, I've grown comfortable being alone but I never want to completely isolate myself. Throughout my experiences, I've become slightly more guarded and picky with who I associate myself with but I think that I will always be too loving and kind towards others."

Anonymous #7:

"Personally, I believe my style and who I am as a person today is strongly influenced by the people around me, especially my family. My parents are both very creative people; my mom sews and has created many side jobs by selling her crafts, and my dad is a woodworker. Both their creations have filled our home and my life. While growing up in a very artistic environment, I believe this has influenced me to have a very unique style from others. Even as a kid, I never wanted to dress or look like everyone else. My mom gave up trying to pick out my outfits at a young age because I always wanted to do my own thing. I find myself still like that today. So many times, I find things I like at stores, but instead of buying it, we snap a photo and make it at home instead. This way I can put my own twist on it and also have the satisfaction of being able to say "Hey, I made that!" Though being different is something I've always strived to be, standing out puts you in a very vulnerable state. If you're not like everyone else, society tends to see you as easy prey to judge. Most times, I get many compliments on homemade or unique pieces, yet there's always negative opinions as well. I think this is where lots of my insecurity sprouts from. I'm constantly struggling between wanting to fit in but still wanting to stand out in my own ways. This is part of my personality that is influenced by two groups that surround me: my family who encourages individuality but then society who seems to degrade anyone else goes against status quo.

However, I am also influenced by the people I choose the surround myself, since family and majority of my peers are people who are coincidentally around me. Yet, there is a smaller number of people who I have control over in my life. For example, my boyfriend encourages me to take risks that I normally wouldn't be comfortable with. I'm someone who worries a lot; it helps to have someone to push me that extra step so I can experience different opportunities. Also many of the friends I have met during soccer have made me the hard worker I am today. Personally I believe a little competition makes everyone stronger. By being on a team, I've learned to be determined, focused, supportive and understanding. Furthermore, I take interest in filmmaking. Every student or advisor I've come across in film has offered me new knowledge. The industry has so many different personalities and it takes them all to produce something so amazing. Therefore by being a part of this group, I find myself always yearning to learn more and expand my education in so many fields. The people who I surround myself with have shaped me into the person I am today. Positive or negative, I wouldn't want to change anyone from my past, otherwise I would not be the same person."

5. When you're with your friends what honest emotions do you feel?

Anonymous #8:

"When I am with my friends my emotions are all over the place because they are all different and express different vibes. The reason why is because my group of friends are very diverse. Some of them are drama queens, some are athletes and others are just the average Joe. When I am around my best friends I feel very comfortable and I can tell them anything. On the other hand when I am around my "friends" I can't tell them everything because they might stab me in the back. Some of them like to talk and gossip. So when I am around my friends my emotions vary."

Anonymous #9:

"I would say that I have a lot of friends considering how shy I can be at times. There are different kinds of friends for different experiences but they all make you feel something. There are friends you do everything with and they are the ones who develop new habits from.

There different kinds of emotions that I feel when hanging out with my friends. I feel dishonest. Dishonest because we all feel differently and act/say different things when one person isn't there. I feel bipolar. Bipolar because they make me the happiest but also make me feel the worst, at the same time. I have the most and least patience when it comes to my friends. They say patience is key and that's all you need but those are lies. I mean fuck, you need everything in you not to break down and lose your mind. Why is it that we all have made the best memories when high? That is the only time we're not bored and really fucking fuming with the light in us, we're unstoppable. But then we come down from our high and we start to lose patience from a long day and it's suddenly all vs. one again."

6. How do you think people perceive you?

Anonymous #10:

"I'm perceived as a young juvenile because I'm Hispanic. I've had a teacher in middle school tell me his first impression of me was mediocre but in the end, I had proved him wrong. There are always bad people in every culture and for my culture we are all perceived as "hood rats or cholos" all we do is deal drugs or rob stores. We are good for nothing low life's. It definitely got worse when

Trump came along. My grandparents came from poor families and worked their ass and risked everything to come into America just for their kids' sake and to have a better life. My parents did the exact same living poor in this country and just trying to get by. The fact that my grandparents and parents worked so damn hard just to be called "wetbacks" is fucking ridiculous. Hispanics work hard and do all the dirty work that privileged people don't want to do like picking oranges or construction. We are good people, yes there are Hispanics that go down the wrong road but there are people in every race that do that. We don't deserve that discrimination and stereotypes. I'm proud to be Hispanic because I know what goes on in a Hispanic household. I know the blood, sweat, and tears that my grandparents went through and I can only look up to them. They should be respected for what they went through not shamed and be told to go back to their country. We are all human beings who should be treated like the humans we are. Compassion is key and in this world we have very little."

Anonymous #11:

"Well for those that don't know me it's easy for them to perceive me as a jock. I was a freshman that started on varsity, I hang out with all classes (senior, junior, etc.) and you can say I'm more on the "popular" side. But for those that know me they know that I'm just a California boy chasing my dream. When I was younger I had friends that got bullied and I hated to see my friends sad or upset. Ever since then my motto was that "No one messes with my friends or else they have to mess with me". My goal when I go to a new place that I don't know is to make as many new friends as I can because you never know when you might need a friend or that friend you met might be your boss someday. My friends know that I am just a nice guy with a lot of funny jokes, very blessed to be talented with baseball, have good grades, and lives by his words. Everyone has their own opinion on things so I challenge you to take time out of your day and step out of your comfort zone and meet someone new"

Anonymous #12:

"Realistically, I think people perceive me as outgoing, comedic, and energetic. I come off as outgoing because I have a tendency to put most people before me. I also like to make friends and I can have a conversation with just about anyone. I'm really friendly and I'm definitely a "people's person". I am comedic because I love to have fun and crack jokes. More times than not, you will find people laughing at something stupid that I did or said. Making people laugh, makes me feel good as well because I get to laugh also. Lastly, I am energetic because I'm always running around. I love to have fun with friends. At school dances, you bet you'll find me in the mosh pit. Those three adjectives describe how I believe that people perceive me."

7. Do you think social media has affected you in a positive or negative way? Explain.

Anonymous #13:

"Social media has its perks yet I wouldn't say it has affected me and countless others in a positive way. Yes, social media is great for connecting and getting news from old friends. However, it has brought many unnecessary issues. Whether it be with subtweeting/@ on twitter and causing unnecessary drama that somehow unfortunately one of the only things that people care about nowadays to posting very cruel posts like nudes, violent acts to be humorous like abusing animals, and the list can go on."

After reading, I hope you continue to open your hearts and minds to accept differences, one person at a time.

New Beginnings

If her soul were to be a color
It'd be yellow
There's a sense of comfort when you're with her
Warmth
The energy she gives bounces off of the walls and onto you
She says yes to new experiences
If life gave her lemons she would take them
But is lost in the taste of green bliss
She is fixated on the idea of imperfection and the acceptance of it
And searches for the hidden pieces of her identity within the pages of books
Her story is vibrant and is just getting started

Writing Activity

1. In "Two Faced," Samantha describes the different sides to her personality that may seem different, but are both part of one person. Think about the parts of your personality that are different from each other. Make two lists of characteristics that seem to contradict themselves. Write a poem about the different sides of your personality by describing the different characteristics.

2. Samantha's interviews asks anonymous people deep questions about their experiences. What are some deep questions that you would like to ask the people you know? Make a list of five to ten questions and ask your close friends and family. Record their answers and write a response in a poem about what you learned from those questions.

3. If someone were to make a movie about you starting today, how would that movie begin? What colors, sounds, and images would they use? Write a poem describing the beginning of your movie. Use light, sound, and color to describe the scene.

Jose Vega

Jose was born in the year 2002. He has three brothers and lives with both of his parents. He loves science and engineering. His favorite book series (The Lord of the Rings) inspired him to make this piece by giving it a medieval setting.

One year ago today

One year ago today, the first of June was a day that would change the lives of thousands, a day that marked the fall of many and the rise of few.

On this day a small community occupied by less than a hundred, was overrun by the ravenous minions of a man with immense power, a man whose minions will obediently do anything he asked of them. He fed them propaganda, teaching them to his ways in a new land pushing to overcome the reluctant fighters, who were there first, as has happened many times in human history before.

Every one of these people had their own motives and desires to achieve in this new land. Some were smarter than others and immediately designated teams under their leader to set up bases for supply collection. The naive ones served the smarter forming factions below the ultimate one, under their glorious leader, who continued to tour the land to show all it contained. He portrayed it as a land of milk and honey, yet the members saw little of it.

The fighters of the land quickly strut down their bases. Raw power and guerilla techniques overcoming what they didn't have by way of numbers. Some say that in one battle 3 men slew 400 of the newcomers, but this did not stop the endless waves of brutes who sucked the land dry.

Villages, bases, farms, and sanctuaries sprung at a remarkable speed, the faction leaders working quickly to supply each other. They put together armor and powerful weapons to fight back against the original community. One by one they began to fall whether killed in combat or deserting due to lost hope.

The hundred slowly began to grow weaker, their numbers slowly but surely decreased.

The new comers surged with pride at the terrible deeds that they have committed. The leader's propaganda grew at an explosive rate encouraging the many that came that the original community had declared war on them first, they deserved to die. Hope grew thin as wave after wave of newcomers trampled the once-thriving land.

None had paid attention to the fact that outside of the rich who controlled the operations, that their own men were starving and dying off. Bodies were strewn across the land, falling to exhaustion in the middle of their tracks. Backpacks overflowing with useless items, tree trunks bare from those who desperately ate the last remaining apples outside of the few sanctuaries whose locations had become a secret, the newcomers were dying at a remarkable rate.

However, the leader rich and proud, would not help his people; he would read through the rewards, take the best equipment, that his slaves had to offer, he pushed them to murder what was left of the once called legendary hundred hoping to claim or kill everything that was good about this new land until nothing was left.

The original hundred were no more than just filthy buffoons struggling to survive, their numbers had decreased to just fifty, they were desperate, fear had stricken them. each and every single one of them had slain hundreds even thousands, but they still outnumbered them by a tremendous amount. For every one they killed ten ore joined the fight, for every base destroyed ten more would be erected. Farms, sanctuaries and monuments would be blown to smithereens and yet they were strong, brave and proud, but their inability to continually unleash new attacks was betting the backs and of even their most powerful.

Hope seemed lost, but then during a meeting between the remaining fifty, one man approached with an idea. He had looked closely at the propaganda that the newcomer's leader continually released, analyzing the psychology used to trick his faction into ignoring the death of their friends and keep reaping the fruits of the land with no care for consequence. This man came forward with his own propaganda, a trick that he hoped would turn the newcomers against themselves. He knew that the that all the newcomers wanted to be special like the leader himself, he knew that that they all wanted a designated rank, for their names to be known amongst the land; but not everyone could be noted for everything they had done, and yet each and every one of them desired this special recognition. Because it gave them a chance to be close to their leader. With individuality came a greater chance of getting to directly speak to the leaders, to enter the Thrym and witness the beautiful words that came from his mouth. So the man from the remaining fifty released his project.

The man knew that the fifty were had slayed thousands of newcomers tricking them into thinking that they were part of the fifty.

The man assumed the name for the fifty, he called them the veterans, in the propaganda he said that they were here first the land was theirs, and they would never stop fighting. He promised them a catch if they could join the leadership under the veterans they would be given the rare gifts that only the fifty had acquired. They could thrive, they could be rich, fame would be passed all around, each could finally be special, only if they turned against their glorious leader. When the veteran released his propaganda, it spread instantly like wildfire. The dying took up arms against their friends attempting to convince them to join the war against themselves or risk being murdered. The smarter of the newcomers became spies infiltrating the greater ranks of the faction. The in the quiet of night they would give the veteran leader the location of the bases sanctuaries, monuments the 50 would split and swiftly move from location to location destroying the progress the newcomers made ending their pitiful lives far greater than ever before. Screams rose into every single night now as the fifty tore apart lives. Higher ranks in the faction had their movement plans revealed and would be swiftly assassinated, no one was safe anymore.

The newcomer's leader did finally notice the death at his feet. His numbers had diminished at a remarkable speed, far greater than the rate at which he could get new men onto the land. Fear began to bite into him as the number of men calling for his death grew greater and greater. His minions fought each other relentlessly killing themselves off. His sanctuaries and farms were burnt down. Every day, the leader continued to release new propaganda, desperately trying to rally his troops, but with fear and sickness at all the lower levels of the military he could no longer sweep the world with the strength that he once had. The legendary fifty, these veterans were unstoppable in a fit of rage the leader demanded a duel against the veteran who smote his men with hope. He stormed out of his home guarded by these two strongest men swiftly travelling. Across the land, the veteran leader in a castle the fifty once lived, but now had abandoned. He threw the doors open ascending innumerable floors of the castle it's remarkable architecture kept on imposing him through his rage and after hours of searching the massive structure he arrived at the door of the throne room and told his men to wait outside. He brandished his sword and took a deep breath and threw the door open. At the other end of the halls at the leader of the veterans on his dark red throne grinning wryly at him, crumbling pillars on either side and to the right was an opening to the sky revealing a starling drop to the grassy plains below.

"I'm surprised you actually showed up" his voice boomed from the other end of the firmament. The Faction leader had never heard the voice of the veteran before, it's power shook his bone as it echoed through the empty rooms of the castle. "I gotta say I'm impressed" the leader swallowed, filled with fear. These men were legendary, the blood-stained sword the leader casually held up had killed an innumerable amount of his men. The sly grin on the veteran's face was charismatic and intimidating. It was no wonder he could trick the newcomer's men into fighting each other. The veteran's casual demeanor was an insult to his leadership, his military power; no one should look the newcomer in the eye and not feel fear and yet this man did not. Not only was he void of fear but his casual confidence made the newcomer shake where he stood. For the first time in hs life he felt true fear, his men were at the other side of the door, he could not back down now. "Don't be surprised" he said trying to hide his fear and keep his own intimidating voice intact, "I never back down from a challenge," the veteran stood, the grin never veered from his face. His dark eyes piercing the newcomer's soul. He walked forward his footsteps echoing through the once thriving castle. So he looked the newcomer directly in the face. He extended his hand offering to shake on a pact of goodness. In this land fairness did not exist but the veteran knew if he truly wanted to beat the newcomer he would need to convince his minions that he'd won fairly and without deceit. Their hands touched, the newcomer flinched at the icey coldness of his hand, a hand that had strangled so many of his own men, the hand that gripped the sword that doomed his entire army. Bitterness and hatred filled the newcomer as he stared the veteran in the eye.

Finally, he wrenched his hand away and turned to take a few steps back. Fate watched over them as they looked each other in the eye one last time and final moment of peace. Both knew that only one was going to live. They charged at each other with agile movements swiftly striking each other. They both struggled to maintain control each fell back, they struggled, screaming insult after insult. For hours they fought, then in one fatal blow the veteran struck the faction leader through the chest. He screamed in agony, his screams were heard all the way throughout the land. Everyone knew that the war was just ended. The veteran leaned over and said, "I'm sorry" then at that point the newcomer took his last breath and said, "me too."

Stereotypes

Why do you hate us so much.
Why do you blame us
Why?

We came for opportunity,
Happiness,
We came for a place to call
home

We come over
We look for Jobs
But end up with the
Same jobs from before

construction, landscaping
factory workers
farmers and ranchers

We come not given a choice
Of what we want

You see us as stupid
Or
Unacceptable of doing other things

We live in poverty
Because we are
Not give a
Chance

We come for opportunities
We come because we
Know that we are
Capable

But we try
We get separated
We get overlooked

We are seen as the problem
The inferior
The workers
But
We know that we can do more
And you too know this

Why do you hate us
Why do you blame us

There is no need
For a wall

Why, America, Why?

Writing Activity

1. Jose credits *The Lord of the Rings* for inspiring his epic tale, "One year ago to-day." Stories of heroes and warriors, battles and deaths, good triumphing over evil (in the end) are common themes in epic tales because they draw us in with their rising action, keep our attention with twists and turns, and ultimately give us hope for a "happy ending." Write your own epic tale --- include characters such as warriors and battle leaders; include battle scenes and dialogue between the fighting forces; include a moment when "all seems lost" for the heroes and a moment when it all "turns around" and the "happy ending" comes for those who are good.

2. Jose's poem "Stereotypes" shares personal feelings of hurt, confusion, and rejection in response to xenophobic* events/policies that were targeting him and people like him in the months following president Trump's 2016 election. As writers we often write questions that need to be asked, that need to be thought about, but that we may never get to hear the answer to. Write a response to Jose and others like him who ask, "Why, America, Why?"

*Xenophobia is defined as "intense or irrational dislike or fear of people from other countries."

Tony Robertson

The child of a single mother, the woman that I worship. My life belongs to her, the most inspiring person I know. In my own personal diary, she's my ambition. She takes care of me, even when I want to be a stubborn kid. She's one of a kind. Life created the greatest masterpiece that ever walked on the surface of the earth. My BIO has been recognized by her creation, her son.

My letter of apology

Hi this is to you the ugly girl
This is to you the fat girl
This is to that dumb girl with bad grades
This is to the sick girl
This is to the girl who could never find love
This is to the girl with the beautiful broken smile
This is to the girl who lives with creeping hands at night
This is to that girl who hurt just so hurt emotionally and physically damaged
My letter to all of you women… (pause 3 or 4 seconds)
Listen I don't know your story and I just wanna stop this poem talk to you real quick if you don't mind
Although I can't be there for you physically who says I can't be there mentally? You probably haven't heard this in life but your beautiful and no not your physical appearance but your halo… your halo is shining bright and im sorry that no one Is there to tell you that your one of a kind… but you are… so don't ever think that you should lower yourself to no other human… because it you no nobody is better than you …you have a story that your making because every legend starts somewhere …so smile bc ima be here when you wanna talk

Writing Activity

1. Tony writes "My letter of apology" to several types of girls --- girls he doesn't know and may even never meet, but still feels that they deserve to hear the words of encouragement he has to say to them. Think about who you "know about," but may not know, that needs to hear words of encouragement and write a letter of apology to them.

2. Tony's "My letter of apology" is written to girls he never expected to hear from, but that he wanted to encourage to tell their story. Imagine you are one of the girls he is writing to and write a letter back to him --- let him know your story, let him know what you want to talk about.

Evelyn Bahena Casas

My name is Evelyn Bahena Casas. I'm currently going to Sunny Hills High School. My birthday is on August, 17, 2001. I'm a pretty shy person when you first meet me, but once you get to know me better, I'm honest, trustworthy, and helpful however I can. I'll comfort you with my words when your world is falling down because honestly, negativity is so horrible. At my house, there are some rules, but the ones that stick out to me the most are, "family first, then friends, we all matter," and the other one is a quote: "A Smile is contagious, so say cheese."

Usually I'm not that busy, but yeah, I hate getting bored so I try to find something to do like go for a walk with my dogs, ask a friend to skateboard with me, play Just Dance, or watch Netflix, which is one of my favorites. In my high school during lunch time, there's always a big line so instead I bring lunch or just go to the snack cafeteria. Then I go to clubs that I sign up for, which are Anime Club and Happy Feet Club that helps out the pups and kittens. Who wouldn't want to join? They're so adorable. In the Happy Feet Club, you pick a kitten or a pup, then you take care of him/her while trying to find an owner to take care of him/her.

What's my favorite class? Well, it's 3-D design class because you basically use your hands, creative imagination, and wait, one more: your heart, which is important. You use your hands for everything. They're your tools to everyday life. We use technology every day for everything like work, projects for school, sharing your information, or just for entertainment. Well, honestly, I use it more for the entertainment: for movie night, watching hacks, music to calm you or for a party. It's all just so amazing, what we can do with technology. We can even save our planet.

Brother

We're all humans, right we all have problems they're not all easy to solve so let me tell you something my brother is both generous and kind but his friends are mostly cholos. One day I see my brother sitting on the chair outside with a pack of cigar's smoking. I ask away saying "why are you smoking" but doesn't answer so I walk back in. Few years later he meets the love of his life he doesn't smoke anymore at least that's what I thought. Few days after his wedding one of his old cholo friends shows up looking all professional but don't let the looks blind you. What happens next angers me he pulls out a box of cigars. I come in behind take the box but my brother shouts at me saying "Necesito Ese Cigarro."

Writing Activity

1. Has someone close to you ever disappointed you? What did they do and why did it matter to you? Write a poem about what happened and how you felt.

2. Have you ever spoken up to someone older than you? Why did you speak up to them? How did they react? Write about what happened and why you chose to speak up.

3. Try reading one of your writing pieces out loud to a friend or family member. Ask them to close their eyes while you read so they can focus on your voice and words. When you finish, ask them what they saw, heard, or felt while they were listening. How does your voice add to the meaning of your words?

Sophie Johnson

Sophie Johnson is a nerdy girl who loves anime and animals. She attends Rockport Fulton Middle School and wants to be a veterinarian when she grows up. She plans to go to Texas A&M University in College Station and is very outgoing.

Free but Unwanted

Aquamarine's scales glistened in the eerie moonlight. Black water rushed by her body. Legs, arms, and lungs aching with a dull pain. Riots formed on boats behind her chasing relentlessly. "Kill the Dragon!" they shouted. Through the earsplitting yells of the villager and the loud splashing of the water nobody could hear the teardrops crawling their way down her face towards the water. Years of isolation only to be greeted by rejection and violence.

Soon the, what seemed to be endless lake, came to a close. She dragged herself out of the lake, water cascading down her body. Overworked muscles rippled underneath her skin burning with the effort. She flopped down onto the marshy grass not caring about the boats of rioting villagers behind her. People came flooding out of the boats whooping in victory. She sighed in defeat. People closed in on her threatening her with mesmerizing fires and jagged sticks stained crimson from past hunts. Memories flooded through her mind stopping at one she had forgotten long ago. One of her mother teaching her a spell only to use in life threatening emergencies, as the effects were irreversible. Ancient dragon language escaped her mouth. Air swirled around her knocking anyone in close proximity away. Out of the mini tornado stepped a beautiful young woman with milky skin and hair matching the color of seaweed. She took one last look at the villagers and ran away to the horizon cloak swirling in the wind. Soft grass tickling her feet. She was free! She smiled a sad smile. She was free, but she was still unwanted.

Snapped

Dark

Black

Everybody cares. Everybody.

Stop

lying to yourself.

Nobody cares. Nobody.

Laughter in your head.

Taunts you. Mimics you.

You're being bent in half but you're still holding on.
Everybody's staring. Staring at you.
What did you do wrong?
Everything. Everything's wrong with you.
Soon the laughter in your head will become a reality.
Oh wait, it already has.
The stares that burn you in your mind will soon start to sting
in real life. Oh
wait, they already have.
The wildfire that's burning through your sanity will spread until there's
nothing left. Oh, but wait,
it already has.
You're bending farther than you've ever been bent.
Cracking away at the edges.
A loud SNAP can be heard from miles away.
Except nobody's here. Nobody cares.
You're falling. Snapped in half.
Arms flailing.
You did it. You snapped.
Isn't that what everybody wanted?
No it wasn't.
But now you're just falling.
Waiting, to hit the ground.

Hope

"Bye, Mom!" I walked out of the door of my apartment.

My mom is terminally ill with cancer and has almost no chance of surviving. I put on a smile every day so nobody knows the pain I go through. Every time I see her it feels like daggers through my heart because I know I might not ever get to see her again. What pains me the most is that when I am at school she could be suffering, and I would never know. She never tells me when she's hurting, not even if it means she could die.

But I have Hope. Hope that she will get better. Hope that she might, just might not, die. Hope that she is strong enough to get through this.

Images flash before my eyes. My mom as she goes to the doctor. My mom as she gets her first wig. My mom finally being greeted with the amazing news that she is cancer free. Then, most importantly, my mom wrapping her petite arms around me.

When I felt the warmth from her hug, it occurred to me that these were not just images from my dreams, but were now our reality. Maybe Hope does pay off?

Writing Activity

1. Think about an issue that you have experienced in your life. How did you feel about it? How did you deal with it? Write a story where a creature – it can be real or mythical – faces these same issues and feels the same things you did.

2. Sounds have strong connotations and can carry meaning for us, such as in the poem "Snapped." Think of an interesting word with a unique sound; maybe it's something you say or have heard in your life. Write a poem using this word and describe how it makes you feel.

Kasia Driver

Kasia Driver was born on September 16th, 2004 and lives with her mother, father, and older sister. In 3rd grade, she won 2nd place in a writing contest in Tyler with her poem "In The Meadow." She plays the bassoon in her school band and is the McMichael Middle school mascot.

Eyes Of Gold

Arms embracing
Heart of fire
They always see you
In times of dyer

I will not let them go untold
I'll Tell the world of your eyes of gold

They seem to always shine
Through struggle and hardship
Hate, regret, crime, and war
They see the love regardless

They are priceless, they won't be bought or sold,
Forever yours, your eyes of gold

You feel alone
Like no one is there
But they see and feel for you
Because they care

I know I envy what you hold
But they are yours, your eyes of gold

They make me feel
As im no longer weak
They see through everyone
What do they truly seek?

I will not lie, the truth will unfold
I will forever love your eyes of gold

Writing Activity

1. “Eyes of Gold” is a poem that focuses on one part of the body. It describes the eyes in great detail, including the way they look and their effect on other people. Try writing a poem or a short essay that focuses on one part of the body: your hands, your hair, your shoulders, perhaps.

Go back and re-read “Eyes of Gold.” Look closely to see when rhyme is used and when it isn’t used. Also pay attention to Kasia’s use of repetition of the phrase “your eyes of gold.” Go back and look at your poem or essay and think about whether and how it might enhance the piece to repeat key phrases periodically.

Tytrice Conor

Tytrice Conor is 14 years old. She is from Lubbock, Texas, and she likes to play sports. She is interested in dancing and singing.

On Silence

When I was in the 4th grade I came to stay with my dad for the summer. I thought I was going to be able to go back home with my mom, sisters, and family. Instead without me knowing, my mom and dad made an agreement that I was to stay with my dad for a semester. I didn't want to but since I was only 9 or 10 years old it wasn't my choice and I really didn't have a say in the situation. I was real sad and I was very upset. I would cry every night because I was separated from my family. I had to get used to a new environment and new people. I didn't like it all because it was all surprising and I wasn't used to this feeling. It was the worst feeling of my life. If I could go back in the past and say something, I would want to say that I did not like the choice that my parents had made, and I wish it was my decision to make my own choices when I was younger. I'm actually happy I experienced this because now I know that it is important to speak up and speak my mind because now I'm older and they will listen to my thoughts now.

Writing Activity

1. Write about a time when you felt silenced. This could be related to your age, race, gender identity, religion, physical ability, or other identities. If you could go back to that moment, what would you have wanted to say?

2. What activities, people, or places in your life empower you and let you share your voice?

3. Describe several ways that you can support individuals or groups of individuals who may feel voiceless. You may choose to write in the form of a declaration or manifesto.

Jorge Molina

Jorge Molina was born on October 19th, 2003 in Fountain Valley, California. He is an incoming freshman at Santa Ana High School located in Santa Ana, California, and his favorite hobby is soccer. He has a younger brother and an older sister and is unlike the typical middle child. He aspires to study Civil Engineering at Stanford University.

Separation

My Father
Mi Padre
Always there for me, for US
Helped in our struggles
Never gave up no matter how hard
And now only a message can merge the miles between us

My Mother
Mi Mama
When she came back
A huge weight was lifted off my shoulders
When I saw her I felt blissful
But she isn't my dad

I never thought this could happen to me
"You can't travel back to the United States."
That's what they told my dad or something like that

I had to leave him
I was alone,
I was with my sister
I was devastated at the time
Because I did not know when my dad would finally be with me
I felt the pain that other families who have been separated before felt.

Writing Activity

1. Being separated from family is a traumatic experience that many people in America face. Jorge explores this through his devastating poem. Have you experienced something bad that affects you to this day? Try writing a poem to help you explore it. You don't have to show it to anyone. Sometimes healing needs to be personal, and that's ok.

Eduardo Jose Gutierrez

On August 26, 2001 a big, chubby baby was born. His name was Eduardo Jose Gutierrez, son of a brilliant mom and talented dad. He was born into loving science, soccer, and DC Universe characters. Although soccer is the sport he is best at, he would love to play basketball, even with a dry shot. Now when it comes to report card grades, science seems like it isn't one of his strongest subjects, but he can somewhat tell you the definition to Einstein's relativity theory, thanks to National Geographic; yeah, he gets a bit nerdy. DC Universe is the world to him, especially when that world has his top 2 favorite characters, the Flash and Batman. Yeah, it may seem childish, but I mean, who doesn't like superheroes? He seems like an amazing guy, wants to live big and has goals to set. He always tries to keep a smile on his face, even if his past or present haven't always been the best, but something tells me his future will be just fine.

Freedom

Freedom is like a goal
Not reached by the goalie.
Many say it's easy to reach
But is that true?
8-inch ball representing
Freedom
It's pretty hard to reach.
Trying to grip on
To freedom,
Is trying to get
The last plane ticket
To leave a world
Of war.
No matter the way
I try to state the point,
It all comes down to say
Freedom is just another thought.

Writing Activity

1. Eduardo, in his biography, defines himself through likes and activities. How do you define yourself? Write a biography by making a list of your likes, activities, and personal history.

Ashley Beltran

Ashley Beltran was born on February 10, 2001. She lives in Santa Ana where she currently attends Godinez Fundamental High School. She wants to give credit to her sister, Denise Beltran, for encouraging her to do Barrio Writers.

Stuck in the Labyrinth

I wake up on a cold silent day, where I gaze upon some words leaping across my mind. What have I lost? Is the word lost, lost in itself? The only thing I have lost is passion. I stand confidently on a stage, where the audience wonders: "Who is she? Who is she trying to impress?" The audience sees right through me. I carry this false image, pretending to be a different person. As the bright light shines. The audience looks dark. The faces of the people become a blur. Everything is fading away, and suddenly no one is there. I see nothing, but pitch darkness. A voice echoes in the empty darkness; dance, dance, dance. Movement does not lie. I cannot hear the music. I cannot hear anything… I lost what I loved most. And here I am in the labyrinth, seeking to find the true meaning of dance. Where one person can express herself in a phenomenal way in a place of honesty and truly experience this form of art. The truth will set you free, and maybe my truth will liberate me from this labyrinth within myself.

Writing Activity

1. Ashley seems to be writing in a stream of consciousness, a form of writing where you try to capture the process of thinking on paper. Try it. Write a piece where you just write down anything that comes to mind. Don't worry about whether it makes sense or not, just write. See what happens!

Lindsey Thompson

Lindsey is an 18-year-old student at Texas State University in San Marcos, Texas. She is pursuing an English degree, and her current life plan is to "wing it and hope for the best." She grew up in El Paso, Texas where she spent most days reading, writing, and cuddling animals. Although she is primarily interested in writing novels, she has recently taken an interest in poetry.

Trapped

Color coding children
From the moment we know
Their genitals

Before they are even
Free of the womb

It's normal, fun
Cut the cake-

Is it blue or pink?

Act like a lady.
Cross your legs and
Braid your hair
Don't play rough or
Think too hard
Cook and
Clean and
Pop out ten kids
Want to work? Sure!
But still do the rest
As well

Be a man.
Stiffen that lip and
Stand up straight
Don't shed a tear or
Feel a thing
Have muscles and
Money and
Be up for a fight

Want to stay home?
Why? Wife got you
Whipped?

Entire lives
Confined and dictated by these
Weighted constructions
Each generation continues to reinforce
With no room for fluidity

Purple doesn't exist
Not to these rules.

But life is a
Spectrum
Purple exists
And Turquois
And Mauve
And Hazel
And Yellow
And none of these
Exists purely alone

Stardust

I am a star: a white dwarf
The nuclear reactions inside me
Once hold the universe at bay
But now have given up
So only an ember flickers at my core
I can't push back on gravity as it condenses
and condenses
and
con
den
ses
me
Into a tight ball supported by pressure alone
And I suffocate against the weight of the universe

Forgotten

She says hello and smiles
i say hi
Its' polite
But i do not know her
She says she is my daughter
i shake my head
No
i do not know her

She smiles sadly
"She's gotten worse," she tells another.
i don't know what she means
i don't know why she's here
i do not know her.

i Hate that i don't know her
i Should know her
i think…

i don't know

She brings me to a piano
"Play," she says
i don't know how
"Look." She taps the keys
i don't know.
i tap a key
And another
Another

There is music
It's my hands moving
But i don't know how.
i stop.
She claps and smiles
i don't know why

She hugs me
"Bye mom. I'll see you next week."
She leaves.
i wonder who she is

Writing Activity

1. Define persona. Discuss the difference between personification and persona. Give examples of different types of persona poems. Discuss with writers why it is important to not alienate, stereotype, or caricature the persona with which you're invoking. Empower the writers to be as creative as possible—they can give a voice to a house, a street, a dog, or anything they want.

2. Brainstorming: Try to think about someone who has a life story which sticks out in your mind. Remember, it doesn't have to be a person—your persona poem can be about a person, place, or thing. Your poem could be the persona of a fictional or nonfictional character. It could be about something or someone which exists in a book you read or has had their name appeared in a news article. What is their name, gender, occupation, sexual orientation, their story, etc.? Once you've chosen someone or something, give yourself the permission to imagine their thoughts. Imagine being them. As you begin writing, use "I," the first-person pronoun, to enter into the persona of this person, place, or thing. Where would they go? What would they want to tell you?

Ari Scroggins

Ari Scroggins was born in Galveston, Texas to a then single mother. They are a writer who takes inspiration from the amazing writers around them, including Ashley Ferrell, Christine Mcdermott, and Armani Scott. They draw heavily from fairy tales and childhood nursery rhymes, aiming to repurpose them to have a more modern meaning and application to life. They aim to move others with their writing in the hopes that other students can learn from their experiences and relate.

Tail, Back, and Nose

I ride his coattails, the kind fox
who rescues me. I'm heavy, he tells me,
so I slide up to rest against his back.
He's hot here, his skin radiating
warmth that chilled me to the bone.
I shudder, but I don't move.

The car bumbles along the street,
signs racing past our window,
but I feel syrupy slow in his
passenger seat. He's sweet
like gingerbread and toffee,
and I'm his gumdrop button.

I'm too heavy for his back
he tells me, so I climb onto
his nose. It's rough and wet,
but I can't imagine ever leaving
here. It's painfully silent. Then
the world tilts and I am devoured

Inferno

It was born of ash and fire
with molten skin and liquid lava
lips that dripped scarlet flames
whenever they parted. It was aberrant
to the cool cerulean sea it declared
its home. Fish flee in schools, sharks

stay on bets. Who can last two minutes
with the burning mountain?

His sharp canines bite at its side, seeking
submission from the dangerous being
who dared to resist. Boulders fly
from his jaws, chipping at its skin
to devour its essence. Let him bite
away. Let his fangs sink into flesh.
Let him pillage and plunder its
body, because it is a goddess.

It is so much more than mere rock
and steam. It is a conflagration.
It is an explosion that cannot conform
to simple adjectives. It is more than beauty.
So come. Eat it's bread which is given for you.
Drink its blood which has been spilled for you.
Seek deliverance for your crimes, because She
is forgiving. She is all that is and all that were.

Do this, not in remembrance, but in praise.
For She will not stand to be forgotten.

Stasis

He lay there, the bed his tomb
a clear glass casing that threatened
to hold him in stasis until his death.

Skin pale as egg shells and slate
grey eyes that have not opened
in months. His face a mere shadow.

She sits beside him, his hand clenched
in her fists and she presses her lips
to his skin, an act of desperation.

It's their last sunrise, the hues
shining on the silver machines
that beep away his life.

There she comes, the woman in white,
hand on the plug, as he opens his eyes.

Green

it was no one's prince.
it would never be leading
man. its skin wasn't faire
and his eyes were black,
beady abysses that refused
to entrance even the lowliest
of maidens. it was the frog.

A grotesque, green monstrosity
that lurked in dark corners
and stole glances at forbidden
treasures. it was an aberration,
condemned by the so-called court.
it was a wrinkle in the delicate
fabric of society's image of perfection.

But He, whose eyes shone
with such a fierce light,
and laugh that parted seas.
He who was pure, held a flame
that burned away its warts
and washed the green from its skin.

He, whose lips were its own cure
that when placed over the frog's
reminded that it was human too.

Wicked

She is old, her skin a leathered
tapestry. Tough and thick.
She is mad, her mind a twisted
knife, piercing those before
her and those who would come after.

How did this woman become so wicked?

Tell me the story of the red apple
that stole her trust. Her very mother
who stole years and attempted to end
her life with a bitter sweet bite.

Tell me of her brother, the trusting
fool, traipsing through the woods
in search of gingerbread and frosting.
The kind stranger who smiled
and then stuffed him in an oven.

Tell me the story of the prince
who stole her innocence with a kiss.
The sleeping princess, peaceful and
serene, shaken awake by grasping
hands and desperate cries.

Tell me not of her actions.I know
them all; the once innocent woman
who transformed the slick-haired prince
into a slippery frog. Remember,
the truly wicked never began as such.

Writing Activity

1. Ari mentions in their bio that they strive to repurpose childhood fairy tales. In "Tail, Back, and Nose," Ari alludes to the story of the Gingerbread Baby --- in some versions the Gingerbread Baby gets away from the fox at the end, but in other versions (like Ari's), the Gingerbread Baby is not able to outrun the sly fox. Think about the obstacles (figurative and literal) that you experience in your life. Consider the outcomes of experiencing those obstacles (actual and wished for), and repurpose a fairy tale to tell your own tale --- with a happy or devastating ending.

2. Once again, in "Wicked," Ari alludes to the influence of fairy tales on their writing and poses a thoughtful question of "How did this woman become so wicked?" or as they claim, "...the truly wicked never began as such." Think about the "wicked" people you know (real or fairy tale) and write a biography that explains their beginnings and how it has created them to be the person they need to be today.

Za Khia KeIzhane' Davis

Za Khia by definition means peaceful or tranquil, typically what she tries to portray in her poetry. Her love for poetry began in elementary school in the fifth grade. Za Khia went to UIL with a poem she had written all by herself and won first place in the Oral Reading UIL. From then on, she knew poetry would be something grand to her, and in her life she knew she had to prove it.

Born and raised in Nacogdoches, Texas, Za Khia grew up in a pretty suburban neighborhood. She, at the age of ten, realized that if she didn't speak for her people … no one would. She wrote several poems over the years, her favorite one being "In the eye of Judgement," a poem she had written at age 12, about stereotyping other races that we are not familiar with based on some of the people we have heard about from that specific ethnicity.

What do you see?

When you look at me what do you see,
A black girl walking in a class full of whites and everyone turns and looks at me,
Please tell me what do you see,
The teacher talks about slavery and all the white kids look at me…,
What do you see?
A kid that will never get a college degree of a PhD,
What do you see,
An angry black woman who's incapable of doing big things…,
Please tell me what do you see…
Or maybe I should let the light reflect on me…
Or maybe I should forget what you say and tell you what it feels like to be me…,
It feels like I am not free,
Like I am a black person hanging from a tree,
But in reality I am a queen and I truly have a dream,
I am Pro-Black, not Anti-White no matter what it may seem,
So please my white sister…tell me what you see?

A Racist Prom

"Dude , my dad is so not going to let you take my sister to poem", Adam said to Corey. "Why not…we have been dating for almost 6 months" Corey said. "He….he's just not going for that alright!?" Adam said looking Corey up and down shaking his head. "I have to go man…I will talk to you later" Adam said as he sped away down the hall. Months had passed and Amanda had bragged to her family about how wonderful her date was and tonight they would finally meet him. As Amanda finished up her makeup the doorbell rang…Amanda knew it was her date…Corey. Her father, Aaron, opened the door and a look of confusion spread across his face. " Who are you" Aaron asked the 6 foot tall brown boy. "I am Corey and here to take Amanda to Prom, sir". Just as he said that Amanda walked downstairs. " No you are not my daughter will not be going out with someone like… you". A frown appeared on Amanda and Corey's faces. "Why not daddy?" an obviously confused Amanda asked. "AMANDA!" her father scolded "Why would you bring this…drug dealing trash boy into my home?" "Woah no need to disrespect me, you don't even know me sir" Corey spoke. "I know all about your kind boy, what are you a drug dealer, a murderer, the next nigger to get killed by a police officer?" "No, actually I have 6 colleges calling offering full ride scholarships for my grades, they extremely happy to have a drug dealing nigger walking around their campus…now come on Amanda."

Writing Activity

1. In the poem "What do you see?," the speaker asks the question "what do you see?" and then gives stereotypes about black women, such as a lack of education or being an angry black woman. She then tells the speaker how these stereotypes make her feel. Have you ever felt like you were being unfairly labeled? What are some of the labels that others have given you? How did you feel?

2. Why do you think Amanda did not tell her father that Corey was black? Do you think she left with Corey? How would you have responded to the father? Consider writing about an experience you had when you withheld information from your parents or a teacher. Why did you do it? Did it turn out the way you had hoped?

Brandon Spigner

Brandon Spigner is a 14-year-old actor from Dallas, Texas. Brandon has been acting since he was 8 years old. He likes to play basketball and write in his free time.

The Struggles of the Active Child

Stop giving us homework! We all have lives too and don't have time to finish ALL OF IT, and then you complain about how its too much to grade when all YOU have to do is not assign the work. That way it's a win-win for us all.
Let us be LOUD. Let us TALK. Without being told "you're disturbing the peace"
Teachers are cool but homework and being quiet 24/7 isn't S M H!
Students we MUST fight for our rights! Not just the ones I mentioned, but also better food and no uniforms. Teachers please take our advice and
Chillax.
Just chill like the weather in Alaska and me personally want you all to let kids be kids.

Writing Activity

1. Brandon uses phrases like "S M H" (shaking my head) and "Chillax" in this piece. Phrases like this are considered colloquial English, because they are used in every day conversation and aren't considered "formal." What colloquialisms do you use frequently in your speech? Do you use them in your writing? Why or why not?

2. "Let us be LOUD. Let us TALK." Brandon says that teachers are cool, but he takes issue with feeling silenced by his teachers. Have you ever felt restricted or silenced by authority figures at school? What about outside of school? Are there things in your life that feel diminishing instead of encouraging? Write a piece directed towards that person or group.

3. At the end of the piece Brandon, has a call to action for his fellow students: "we MUST fight for our rights!" Is there a cause you believe in that affects you personally? What rights are you fighting for? Write a piece with a call to action at the end of it.

Gabriela Garcia

Gabriela Garcia is a sixteen-year-old Latina from Santa Ana, California. She's a 1st generation Mexican-American who aspires to do big things in her life. She is an outspoken and argumentative person who often wins her arguments due to her persistence. Because of this persistence, she has found a voice: a voice that she often uses to stand up for what she believes in. With her newfound, voice she hopes to aspire and empower others to find their voice just as she did.

No Soy Lienzo, Soy Mujer

Ser mujer para mí es casarte, tener hijos, cuidar la casa, hacerle de comer a mi viejo, cuidar a todos los de más y en fin renunciar a mi vida libre. Desde niña, me metían esas ideas en la cabeza. Eso es lo que siempre se ha esperado de mí. Te digo que ser latina es algo tan hermoso y mágico, nada se compara con nuestro idioma, nuestras tradiciones y nuestras comidas. Y aun que amo ser latina y todas las tradiciones que vienen con ser latina a unas cosas que no me laten. La idea de tener que casarme y renunciar a mi vida es algo que no me caí. Perdón mama, papa, abuela, abuelo, tío, tía, padrino, madrina, perdónenme, pero yo no quiero esa vida que ustedes me pintan. No soy lienzo. Soy mujer, pero eso sí, soy mujer y soy libre también. No tengo planes de casarme ni de cuidar a mi viejo que acabo, él se puede cuidar solo. Solo les dijo que egoísta no me crean porque egoísta no soy, simplemente soy mujer que quiere hacer las cosas a su manera.

Silent House

One Monday afternoon, I was taking a refreshing shower while using my chile shampoo to wash my hair. The door to my blue bathroom was wide open since I lived with only my dog. Since the door was wide open my dog decided to sit at the end of the wooden door and just stare at me with his brown/green puppy eyes. "Okay Pepeto you're being weird again, all you do when I'm home is stare at me. I understand that you love me but honey even love has its limits and you've reached them." In that moment everything became silent and I realized that I didn't really like the silence. After pondering on the silence for few seconds I came up with an idea. "Pepeto, what if I get you a little sister or brother?" He just wagged his tail and walked away like he always has.

Later that day, after my shower I was sitting on my weird blue hammock thing looking at the nearest dog pounds. After deciding on a pound, I picked Pepeto up, and got into my navy-blue car and drove off to the pound. Walking into the pound Pepeto sniffed his surroundings and wagged his tail a bit. Walking through the halls passing by kennels Pepeto seemed nervous so I picked him up to ease his anxiety. I set him down once we got to the puppy section. I wanted him to choose his companion so I put him back on the ground. After wandering around a little I saw him stop and sniff out a specific kennel so I also looked into the kennel. You can say it was love at first sight because as soon as we both saw her she had us in awe. In this medium sized kennel was a tiny black and brown Chihuahua standing there staring at me with her dark brown eyes. She has tiny legs that fit her tiny body perfectly. She was perfect. She had this small bald looking head and these huge ears that might have been too big for her but nonetheless they still fit her perfectly. As soon as she saw the both of us she started wagging her tail and barking at us and that is when I knew that my house would no longer be silent. My house would be filled with endless play time and really annoying barking.

We got home and she immediately peed on the wooden tile in my living room. "Someone obviously didn't have trouble making themselves feel at home." I said to myself. She explored the 1st floor of the house for about 10 minutes she then started crying because she saw Pepeto go upstairs and couldn't due to her short legs so I had to pick her up and carry her up the stairs. After a few minutes of her exploring the 2nd floor of the house she walked into my room and stood at the end of my bed just staring with those dark brown puppy eyes. "What?" After those words left my mouth she started barking at me. She barked until I grabbed her and put her on my bed. Being on my bed she ran up to my face and tried biting me, after attacking me she decided she wanted to be cute and snuggle up in the crook of my neck and fall asleep. I was lying there for an hour with a damn dog on my neck. While we bonded, which was just her sleeping, I decided that the name Peppa would suit her.

After two months with Peppa, she and Pepeto bonded and were the best of friends. They would fight and run after each other every time they got the energy to do so, which would annoy me from time to time but it was also nice to see my shy and asocial Pepeto finally get along with another dog. My little babies were so happy together, even though people would often think they hated each other they didn't know what I did; they chose each other.

Wednesday, June 29 started off as a regular day. It was bright outside with no signs of clouds. It was a beautiful day, or so I thought. I was in the living room on the blue hammock seat thing catching up on some work when all of the sudden I hear one of my neighbors call out for me. His voice was loud with a hint of panic in it. I walked as fast as I could just not fast enough. I get outside and my neighbor tells me that she was hit by a car and that she was gone. I heard every word that he said but I didn't understand what SHE had to do with me, I didn't know what SHE he was talking about until I looked at what he was standing over. As soon as I saw the black and brown colored coat I instantly know what SHE he was talking about. My little Peppa laid there, warm but lifeless. She was laying there like she would when she slept, on her side and with her eyes closed. She was brought into my house and I couldn't help but weep at the sight in front of me. A towel over her body as if she was under a blanket, Pepeto recognizing her scent the moment he walked into the room. Wagging his tail as he walks towards where her scent led him, he stopped, approached slowly and sniffed around just like the first time; her in her kennel and him in the hall, her in her resting place him in this silent house. It sounded the same as it did before her. Silent. The silence was no longer a nice silence. It became a wallowing and grieving silence. A house that once held three now holds two. It was silent. My house was the one thing I didn't like, silent. My house was once again silent.

Writing Activity

1. Does society expect you to behave a certain way because of your gender, culture, class, or some other reason? How do you resist society's expectations of how you should behave? Write a letter to someone in your life about how they expect you to act and how you want to act.

2. In "No Soy Lienzo, Soy Mujer," Gabriela writes in Spanish. Do you speak more than one language? Have you ever tried writing in both languages? What differences do you notice when you write in English as opposed to other languages? Do you display different parts of your identity or character in different languages?

3. In "Silent House", Gabriela writes about the uncomfortable silence in her home. Have you ever felt that something or someone was missing from your home or your life? How did the silence affect you? Did you try to fill the silence with something or someone? Write a story describing a particular silence that you have felt, whether it made you content or uncomfortable, and what descriptive imagery helps illustrate the feeling.

Descriptive imagery is writing that engages the senses and describes a place in such a way as to make the reader feel like they are experiencing what the writer describes. Imagery can help a reader feel the emotions that a writer wants to express.

Eliana Rodriguez

Eliana Rodriguez is a sophomore who has been creating art since she was in elementary school. She is now pursuing becoming an inspiring writer. She enjoys designing characters, creating meaningful art, and is inspired by many authors to create a TV or comic series of her own.

Incinerator

It first occurs as a wave coursing through every inch of my face and striking my heart like a burning arrow. Pressure embraces the bottom of my eyes while the corners soften, now there's a slight bee sting at the bridge of my nose.

My fingers dance around each other in a way that should've left them bent and bruised. I lose the sense in my feet, then my ankles, then my thigh, until I'm unaware of my entire leg being gone. The stinging on my nose is immense, my lungs feel like wax bleeding onto skin.

I wonder if I'm even breathing. My lips are chipped wood but I run through it anyway. I can't hear my throat rattle the remaining air left in my incinerator that was once my lungs. Liquid is burning my vision, tickling my jawline, all the way down my chin. And so I weep with no air left in my frame.

SOL

The very peak of the white rays that consume your house and attack through your blinds is the beginning of my breath and the beginning of your day. Every cloud that covers you from my rays is merely my way of shading you from burning up when I am at my highest reach above you and the rest of the Earth. I do not see myself as superior. But of great responsibility of being your friend.

Every color surrounding your sight turns into the sweetest pink, brightest yellow, and softest blue; until the ends of the horizon. I'm welcoming and calming, I remind you that your day is almost over, that your problems are in the past of today, and yesterday, and the day before that.

Santa Solia

My mother's skin and bones belong within the soils and waters of Mexico. Her very flesh was molded with the fingers of a God and every form and shape of her is from God's nails and fingerprints. The running water making puddles inside the room she was born in was taken to her body where it gave it life. And with God sighing, a child was born in the very soils of and waters of Mexico.

Writing Activity

1. Natural-occurring elements are great objects to use for self-expression. Think of an element (water, fire, rock, wind, space, etc…) and use it to express something inside of you. Try using sensory details so we can taste, hear, see, feel, and smell everything about this element.

2. People can have an effect on us. Whether that be family members, friends, or strangers. They can challenge us, love us, or hurt us. But no matter what it is, a writer can turn it into inspiration. Using any form of writing (flash fiction, poetry, or nonfiction), write about a single person that has influenced you. Describe what they look like and how they have impacted your life.

Crystal Hernández

Crystal Hernández was born in Santa Ana, California on August 20, 2001. She is a junior at Santa Ana Valley High School. She's a 1st degree black belt in Taekwondo, and she is a part of her high school's dance team. Through Barrio Writers, she has explored another art form that she used to explore not only her mind, but herself as well.

Anxiety

I do no harm to you unless you let me
I can't be happy with you around me all the time
I'm only around when something really important matters to you
Exactly why I'm always scared and worried of the outcome
It's not like you have a choice you're stuck with me
Not unless I mute you, you can't control me forever
Or can I? Unless you're forgetting I can come back at anytime and anywhere I'll scream if I have to be heard
But why me? Why do you stop me from growing? Why can't you just let me be happy?
Because you still don't get it, I'm not the one who stops you because the one who does that is you because I'm not real
Sure I may bounce from side to side, I may enter when you need me the least but you must remember I'm just in your M. I. N. D.

Mother – Father

¿Mamá por qué ya no vivimos con mi papa?
¿Papá por qué te peleaste con mi mama?
¿Mamá por qué estás trabajando tanto?
¿Papá porque ya no los buscas?

¿Mamá quién es este hombre y por qué viva con nosotros?
¿Papá quien es esa mujer y por qué viva contigo?
¿Mamá por qué ya no me escuchas?
¿Papá por qué me dices esas cosas?

Mamá ya no te soporto, ya no sé qué pensar de ti
Papá yo te odio no sabes cómo me haces sentir
Mamá por favor ayúdame no puedo con todo sola
Papá apóyame yo no soy una niña mala

Soy su hija, ¿por qué no miran que estoy sufriendo?
¿Por qué no miran que detrás de mi sonrisa es depresión?
¿Por qué no entienden que necesito de su ayuda para ganar esta batalla?
Mamá, Papá que no se olviden que solamente soy humana

Writing Activity

1. In the first piece, the writer used "personification" to write a poem describing anxiety.
Personification is defined as "the attribution of a personal nature or human characteristics to something nonhuman, or the representation of an abstract quality in human form."

Try this writing prompt to create your own personification piece:
Choose one of your flaws, or a characteristic that you think is a flaw, not necessarily something someone can see but it can be physical or part of your personality. Write in the point of view of the flaw, what would it say to you or others? Try to describe its traits without ever stating the name of the flaw. Then share it, and have someone guess your flaw! You might be surprised—people might not even notice your flaw or see it like you do.

2. In the second piece the writer speaks to her parents. If you could write a letter to parents of a teenager what would you say? Try it, write a letter that gives parents advice on how to raise a teen.

Julio Diaz

I'm an English, UTeach, and Creative Writing student at the University of Texas. I am 20 years old. If you ask me "what" I am, I'll simply take a lesson from Whitman and say, "I am large, I contain multitudes." But more so than that, I am queer and brown and a poet born in the south, living in times of peril.

7:21 AM

It is 6:49 am,
And the sunrise isn't for 31 more minutes.

As my desk lamp stays consistent
With its golden beams, my journal is sun kissed.

I know not what to write,
Know not what to speak in plain language.
As depression settles in,
Like a pet curled on your lap,
Or lest it be nuzzled in perch on your neck.
Too calm- adorable.
To do any harm.
Until all they do is nothing.
Curled, or nuzzled.
Gaining in weight,
What no one else can see- lest for you.

They say depression is a sea,
And once you dive in,
It's impossible to swim up.

They say depression is the lull of the night,
The vanishment that happens along with your selfhood.
The silence that is deafening in twilight.

They say depression is overdosing on sleeping pills,
That it is 100 unset alarm clocks,
That it is the day when the sun does not rise,
That it is the night when the moon does not set.

They say depression… well that depression is not normal.
But I think -- but I think,

My depression… And I-
We were meant for each other.

Shorn

Revelation of mothering Flames,
It was she- of triad Shorn
Their glory that had embers igniting inside of us.
Psalms form -- from persisting childhood,
From where blighted lips coaxed of inflamed virtue
Our innocence laid a moment longer-
Being perpetually reflected onto us
In their willful smile.
Psychotic madness derived from absolute sobriety,
T'was choice of her,
Sexual incarnation in awakening,
Ravened Mother,
Purity personed through dutiful slumber
Doting child
Temperate embalming oft. shrewdness.
Resilient Crow.
Lived-in temporal Goddess,
Interacting within us- through
Blessings and charmed melodies,
Sweeping the air in sanctified deity.
Battle saint being no more than an anointment of sacrilege,
And lo, no less than the guide of genesiac thoughts,
As she shifted voices and transformed bodies
To fit the needs of her brightest desires
And darkest necessities-
She left awe in the mouths of those who chose
To follow in cult, and pray to her.

Burning cities once Existed

We were conquerors of the sun and all the flames it had to offer,
Burning with life was our passion,
As children of the equator-
We had lost our sense of purpose,
When all we could do was die out in the vast ocean,
Or lose our breath in the April winds this new land had to offer.

Burning, it is what we were meant to do,
More so brightly than anyone else.
And yet,
We were extinguished,
Out of jealousy for our fires,
We were reduced to suicidal embers,
Edging ourselves with toe dipping's in the waters.
For shining like the stars, we had prayed to,
We were imprisoned to a life without flare,
We limped from matchbox to matchbox,
Always coming to soon with choking,
We never got to breath,
Through these night cities in pitch black,
Prohibited to light a spark,
To see our path,
To see our hope.
Yet-,
We know we'll burn everything to the ground someday.

Flor

I could never pin down her flower,
Always moving from Dandelion
To Daisy to Blue Bonnet and Rose.
I was simple to her,
A volunteering weed-
To make her -- stand out.
Inattentive to her beauty,
She only bloomed on rare occasions.
I-
Her friend in necessity-
Was her nutrition,
When she hadn't figured out how to grow yet,
Where, we thought,
We could change the world.
Nevertheless,
Flowers wilt
And weeds are pulled.
I never did pin down
what kind of flower she was.
I always thought,
Amaryllis

Morning afterglow

A taste of paradise were-
where Women with women
Dance.
And in hidden passageway
Where Boys fiddle with kisses
And roses pricked with romance.
Blaring music resonates,
Washing away our insecurities-
Only to be left with the urge
To dance and sing.
To grow tired and hoarse
From such self-expression,
All tucked away behind a forgotten courtyard,
To be alive.
Next morning, less so alive.
Graying sky painted against that of the traveling windowsill.
As a somber song plays in the background,
Feeding into the white noise,
Minimalistic dancing with fingers and fading smiles,
Happens to be the transit bus
Striding by oblivious workers,
Heading straight down to still rivers,
Sunrise is yet to wake up-
Silver clouds benign in being the only ones in attendance.
Except for you, as alive as you are.
Are present.

Socialized Drug Use

I never understood how children could be so sheltered,
To be ignorant
To the world around them,
They live in this honey soaked illusion,
That the world wants to keep alive,
Just for the sake of knowing,-
Not everything has gone to hell.
But--
Who are they to dismiss-
War,
And

Famine,
And
Death.
Does this great nation have such powers in Death,
That they get to narrate the story that makes them the
Glorious heroes?
Are they able to leave us to become nothing,
But badly drawn caricatures of
Our own selves?
Even we can't wash away the guilt,
For you,
However thick it is in this homeland of ours,
Of how we turn blind eyes,
Turning cheeks to everything around us, leaving us spinning in circles
Have we become nothing but masses looking for the next big
burst of entertaining opiates stemming from social media?
Are we to become addicted to anything that makes us feel good
in this time of broken hearts?

Sight of a Winter breeze

I was not born from the same world as he was,
Smoldering winters and vibrant rainforests
Are what run through the blood of my homeland.
The people of his world consist
Of pale summer eves
And white winter landscapes.
This is not to say, we should never touch,
But rather,
It is better that we do so.
For he has such tender sunset beard,
With polished coal eyes,
And anxious feminine tremors.
Do I do nothing in the presence of such winter glow?
As delicate and frigid as this winter has been for me,
The oncoming scolding summer will be just as harsh for him,
Am I not in obligation to protect the wilting frost
I do see in him?
And him, chill my overheating flesh with
Cool spells and cold fronts from his biting smile.
Such contrast stark to the heavy humidity of this day, that,-
Does this winter fox sitting at gazing sight

In front of me, bring
With matching tie to burning sky.
Our subtle eyes roam each other,
As softened hands caress in memory,
And deflated demeanor comes undone
When existence becomes preferable.

Home

I was here,
Before there was a word
For a place called
Home.
Where poetry was our spoken tongue,
And music was our lullabies,
When love was our martial law.

I was here,
After there was a word
For a place called
Home.

Waiting on you to arrive.

WW

What would
Queer Imagination look like
Without persecution?
What would
Latinx Innovation look like
Without whiteness?
What would
Female livelihood look like
Without sexism?
What would
I –you– look like
Without you –me– ?

The

THE
HET-
EH, T?
THESIS
SISTEH,
ISS HET?
THEATRE!
THE ARTE,
HETE ART-
TE HEART
THEBES,
BE THE S.
THEORY-
THE RYO.

Writing Activity

1. Julio uses metaphors, comparing one thing to another without using like or as, in his poem '7:21 AM,' such as saying "depression is a sea." Write a poem using only metaphors using the template: _____ is a _____. Compare two things and see what comes out!

2. The poem 'WW' asks many questions, all of them regarding the ills in our society such as racism and homophobia. Why ask so many questions? Sometimes, it's ok to just have questions when you don't have answers. Asking any question demands an answer. By posing a question, you force someone to think about what you care about. Write a poem where you only ask questions, no matter how hard or 'absurd' they are.

Adrian

My name is Adrian. I was born in the month of June in the year 2004. I'm 13 years old and facing life obstacles that are difficult to pass through and leave a memory in my head. My experience with writing is not much. This is my first time in *Barrio Writers*, and I've already been successful in the week I spent at the Davis Branch Library. Although I've only visited two countries, my life experience has been amazing.

A Day In My Life

My dad wakes me up at 5:00 A.M to go ordenar the cows. Dad tells me to go put the rope around the cow's back legs while he goes get el cántaro. We stay milking the cow then go back home walking.

Dad gives the cántaro full of milk to my mom and tells her to warm the milk up. I go to my room and use my phone. Once I lay down on my bed-really comfortable-my dad calls me.

I ask, "¿A dónde vamos?"

He says, "Tu nomas ven y ya."

He gets on his horse and I get on my mule. I knew where we were going. We're going to the potrero as known as the woods. It took two hours to get there. Once there, we fed the cows and some horses, sheep and pigs that we have in the coral.

Then we go back home, eat, and rest.

Cada Seis Meses

Yo confronto mi casa,
Me tengo que mover de aquí,
Y moverme a otra casa,
Cada seis meses.

Aquí es temporal.

Confronto la escuela,
Y la tarea,
A veces ay más cosas que hacer.

Esta dificil moverse de casa
Y de escuela
Y empezar de nuevo
Cada seis meses.

The Party

One day, Mexicans made a giant taco party. One Mexican says, "Hey everybody!!! Invite all your friends if you want!!"
And so they all did.
One Mexican invited all his friends including a black kid that was his friend too. Everybody was having fun and all the friends came. The only one late was the black kid. Everybody was eating and dancing. The only one not having fun was the black kid.
His Mexican friend came and asked, "Hey why aren't you having fun with us?"
"I …I … it's because we are different," said the black kid.
"Hey, race don't matter here, we're all friends here and that's why I invited you," said the Mexican.
"I guess," said the black kid. And slowly and slowly he gained confidence with himself and started to have fun with the rest of the kids.

Writing Activity

1. Adrian wrote about a typical day in his life. This form of writing can also be called "journaling." A journal is like a diary or collection of daily events in your life in a notebook. Write "A Day in Your Life" and compare it with Adrian's piece.

2. In his poem titled "Cada Seis Meses," Adrian is referencing his life as a child of a migrant worker in the U.S. (You can use Google Translate to get a general translation.) A migrant worker is a worker who moves from place to place to do seasonal work. For example, the people who pick crops—fruits and vegetables. Most of these workers are provided work visas to pick seasonally and temporary housing, which means they have to move every six months. The move also includes children and youth who attend difference schools every six months. Do you feel the constant moving can be a positive or negative experience for children and youth? Why or why not? If the U.S. didn't employ migrant workers from another country to pick crops, how would that effect the U.S. as a whole? How would this effect the cost of our meals?

Gisselle Lizama

Gisselle Lizama is a 14-year-old Latina from Santa Ana, California attending Valley High school as a freshman. When she is not writing, she is most likely listening to Twenty Øne Pilots, taking videos of her dog, or hanging out with friends.

What Have I Lost? What Have I Gained?

The tears that were traced down my cheeks
when I saw my dog laid down, unwilling to get up
The "friends" I thought would always be there for me
who started to spread those hurtful rumors that teared me apart
The time I spent looking at my phone
waiting as the minutes go by for that one text message to pop up
The money that wasn't used to buy necessary things
I actually needed
The people that I had pushed aside
only to realize later that I wasn't thinking straight

After a while I realized all the things I had lost and I knew I couldn't get back

All the times I tried to spend playing and taking my dog for a walk paid off
I knew how much of a good owner I am
All of the times I spent studying instead of choosing to go out with friends
paid off with good grades
All the practices I decided to go to
paid off by me learning to play a new instrument
All the times I managed to spend as much time with my mom
paid off by showing her how my I appreciate everything she has sacrificed in order for me to have a better future

Writing Activity

1. Sometimes in life we need to reassess what we have "lost and gained" to appreciate where we are in our goals. In response to Gisselle's piece, brainstorm about your "losses and gains" in life and then put them on the page. It can help you appreciate your accomplishments and also plan more goals that work for you—sometimes we just need to list our life experiences to gain a better perspective.

MJ Watson

I'm thirteen years old and born and raised in Nacogdoches. I have four cats, three dogs, and one "bossy" horse. I like cats, books, STAR TREK, and writing. I live with my mom, stepdad, and three younger brothers.

These Colors

These are the colors of the rainforest flowers
Blue, pink, and tangerine.
These are the colors of the rainforest flowers.
Daffodil yellow, lilac purple, and rose red.
These are the colors of the rainforest flowers.
Birds of paradise, lady slippers, and lilies.
These are the colors of the rainforest flowers.
Parrots, macaws, and toucans.
These are the colors of the rainforest flowers.
White, blue, and fiery red.
These are the colors of the rainforest flowers.
Blue, pink, and tangerine.
These are the colors of the rainforest flowers.

Where I'm from

I'm from Oreos and ice cream.
From chase the morning and infected.
I'm from memories good and bad, happy and sad.
From all things blue and gray.
I'm from books and cats.
From my silver tabby tom cat.
I'm from the building stuffed with books, reading whatever catches my fancy.
From mother nature and the ocean blue.
I'm from depression and the midnight wolf.
From the hidden window seat in a secret alcove with a pen and journal glued to my hands.
I'm from Hades abyss, knowing no other name but darkness.
I AM FROM STAR TREK AND GOD.

Epilogue: ME

They call me weird, a freak, nobody, an outcast, weak.
What they say is inaccurate.
They judge me by how I present myself.
If they would just get to know me they would know that I'm sweet, funny, smart, and shy.
These things are accurate.
These are me.

Beast tale (excerpt)

"That stupid witch!" beast roared "who does she think she is to do this to me?!?!" Beast roared, tearing apart the curtains over his bed.

"M-m-master you mustn't work yourself up like this." stammered the candelabra, watching his master tear up his bed.

"Leave at once!!!" beast roared, smashing a table to smithereens.

"Y-y-yes master." Stammered the candelabra, hopping out the door and closing it.

"She said the spell can only be broken with true love." Whispered beast." but who could ever learn to love a monster like me?"

"Master! Its dinner time!" said Mrs. Potts, in a sing-song voice. She rolled into the room and started to pour tea.

"Leave me be." Beast said.

"Now now dear your just hungry." said Mrs. Potts, gingerly handing beast some tea.

"I said leave me be!!" roared beast, throwing the cup of tea against the wall, shattering it.

"Fine. have it your way!" huffed Mrs. Potts, and rolled out of the room in a puff.

"I'm a monster!" roared beast, tearing a family portrait. "this is my fate." Whispered beast in a lonely voice.

Writing Activity

1. In her poem about rainforest flowers, MJ Watson uses a clever writing format of naming colors, naming flower colors, naming flowers, naming birds, and then returning back to just the naming of colors; all the while she includes a repeating line that identifies her main topic. Try to write your own colorful poem in the style of MJ Watson by picking an item in nature, labeling its colors, writing more specific descriptions of its color, transitioning to another item in

nature that connects to your originally picked nature item, and finish off with the colors you originally labeled; and don't forget your repeating line that identifies your main topic.

2. MJ Watson's "Where I'm From" was created in response to George Ella Lyon's poem by the same title. MJ's poem is meant to convey that where she is from goes beyond the city she was born in and includes the memories she has, the people and pets she knows, her favorites, and her fears. To create your own "Where I'm From" poem, take some time to ask yourself a list of autobiographical questions, like --- what are some family nicknames? what traits do I share with my family? what are some of my best memories? what are some of my saddest memories? what makes me angry? what makes me laugh? what are some family traditions? what role does religion play (or not) in my life? what family recipes do I remember most? what songs always make me stop and enjoy long-ago memories? what city/town/country did I grow up in? what language(s) were spoken in my home? etc.

Keep asking yourself autobiographical questions until you have a long list of responses. Next, use the prompt "I am from…" as you pick and choose those memories you want to include in your poem. Mix them up (or put them in chronological order), make them rhyme (or just have incomplete phrases), or just write down a list of your secrets (or explain their meanings).

Fernando Reyes

Fernando Reyes is a 16-year-old writer born in Monterrey Park, California. At the age of 9, he moved in with his mother, relocating to Santa Ana, California. His life is spent between entertainment, writing, and Los Angeles. He has written for the international, teen-oriented publication Affinity Magazine.

The American Dream

Sweating. Miami 1978.

Since as far back as I could remember, I existed. Isn't that true? I don't know. That's the fascinating thing about me, Mariano Capote, my mind isn't fond of much but the adrenaline I pump, or the life I pump, the demons I pump, the ghosts I pump. I was picking up the daily load today, that being blow with vodka, and the ground wouldn't stop moving, so I descended upon the beach, where I met two party girls. Through these two girls, I lived a fantasy; I transported my soul through them and viewed the world. It was a dream within a dream, a fantasy that I desired while living in a reality that was once a fantasy as well. In other words, I was merely going through with my early morning routine, living through others and doing blow on the beach. Sooner than later, I discovered that I wasn't living in another fantasy, I just simply didn't know how to differentiate between reality and fantasy, whatever both of those are, whatever both of those mean. I live in a nightmare. People misunderstand the true meaning of a nightmare, they confuse it with reality, but reality isn't a nightmare, it's a dream, a fantasy, because reality isn't real. Nothing is. People don't seem to understand that.

Fornication. Manhattan 1971.

My catamite lies gently like a sensitive fawn over my Parisian sheets. I purchased them for the very idea of having him lie on them. They worked incredibly well, they draped on his body like silk and he sunk into them as though floating on a cloud. I can't help but to simply kiss him as he rests, his arm, his shoulder, feel his skin, but most importantly, satisfy my intensive need of smelling the Chanel N. 5 that I purchased him. He thanked me rather gracefully for such a gift. He considered it such a gift. I purchased it to him when I first met him at a bar and I've requested for him to wear it ever since the day he dropped everything in his life to be with me, to simply live thinking about meeting me once more, being with me, luxuriating in my presence. He does as instructed, especially for the correct sum of money. Later on we were to visit various penthouses above the city in effort to get him a place of his own, so I could call him whenever so I desired, or vice versa. You see my wife wouldn't be too happy if she ever found this gentle boy on my bed, although I'm assuming Cartier diamonds would reassure her of the frivolous nature of my affairs. The tears on her face won't dry up, but rather they'd run down her face to her neck where every carat would form and would lavishly hang from her body. She's inept; I worry nothing about her, to a certain extent. Give her a credit card of her own and she's gone, she's disappeared. Only, it isn't that simple. I still need her for events and that's where she mustn't find anyone or anything upon discovery... But she's a matter of later. As of now, I'm merely waiting for my boy to awaken, he'll wear his new white rope and we'll eat.

Bawling. Maryland 1945.

My father never returned and I was advised that he'd never do so. I'm not scared but rather confused more than anything. My mother is afraid; she's bawling her eyes out in the kitchen after two men that appeared to be in the military arrived at our front door with the news. I was playing with a helicopter; it was blue with red wheels. I love it very much because of the colors, but most important because it is a helicopter and I am a boy, but I rarely allow myself to think of that. Entertainment can be found in all. Before the men spoke to my mother, I realized I wanted to be like them, tall, heroic and full of courage, but now that they hurt my mother, I don't. Now I see them as criminals, as they hurt my mother when they were supposed to be heroic. As they hurt my mother when they were supposed to be full of altruism. And more than anything, they took my father who was supposed to teach me to play baseball when he returned. I remembered that ever since he told me he was leaving. I didn't like baseball all that much but he bonded with me and loved me in that moment and the love of my father comes first. The way he said it and the way it oozed around my cartilage and into my ear created the most wonderful sound and the most wonderful vibration in existence. That was no longer possible.

Unconscious. Bronx 1983.

I invited my dealer to shoot up with me, as I usually did in my attempt of once again forming some sense of unity, and as it entered my body, I left. I was simply gone. There's this event that took place that was very humorous to me, very ironic. It was as my sore wound reopened for the 4th time that morning and my soul left my body. It was as though something left to make room to something else. I am nothing now because I was no longer alive and a human is nothing without its soul, its mind, its will for existence. Will is created by the soul. It's fascinating but in retrospect, I never saw myself as anything – figuratively, of course. But now it's literal and everyone is afraid of being literal. What depressed me the most about this event was that, as my pupils rolled back, my dealer thought nothing of it. He reached onto my thin, pale, corpse-like body and simply pulled the needle out of my vein, proceeding to insert it into himself. My life rolled back similar to rolls of film playing and I felt absolutely nothing. I was dead; I didn't have emotions because only humans experience such concept, it's why select human beings want no longer to be.

Dapper. Manhattan 1963.

The pebbles on the floor of Wall Street excite every single nerve in me. I have my beautiful, beautiful suit, tailored to mere perfection, with not a wrinkle in sight on and I feel ready. I feel my spine shiver with the thought of finally arriving here, where I felt the need to be, where I'll be made a success story. I was immediately, upon leaving school, offered a job at a very prestigious bank, as an accountant. I don't know where my life will head but I do know that I want to make my mother proud, and, more than anything, I want to make my father proud by supporting the country that he died for. My fiancée Lola supported every way of this move. She took the opportunity of leaving with me as well because of all the rioting that has been occurring. Both Lola and I find protesting to be extremely disgraceful, unpatriotic. There's no sense of respect for the true soldiers who're fighting for our rights oversees. I hope they one day see that. Meanwhile, I will continue my work to better the country that raised me to follow the one and only great American dream. I am the American dream.

Sweating. Miami 1978.

I used to live in reality, I worked 9-5 in my office high on Wall Street, until disco became the flavor and I became tasteless. Needless to say, I have money, and I have some sense of sanity in me. Sanity… that fucking sanity. What the fuck is sanity? I assume its happiness; it's just what I feel. I feel sane. People assume I don't because I dig through the devils frequently shampooed head. Who knew he was clean? I knew he was clean. I wait for him every morning at that alley behind the deli. I see him dressed so dapper and he tells me what I need, the exact same way that I did at Wall Street. He wears a beautiful, beautiful suit, tailored to mere perfection, not a wrinkle in sight. I admire him for that, for presentation, because above everything, presentation comes first, presentation and persuasion is the reason I buy, maybe even add some psychology in there and I find my face numb, although recently, I don't know how to differentiate reality from fantasy, whatever both of those are, whatever both of those mean.

Writing Activity

1. What is "the American Dream?" What does "the American Dream" mean to you? What does it mean to others? Can achieving some dreams have unintended consequences? Write a journal entry about how you or others try to achieve their dreams while living in America. Think about how achieving those dreams might affect you in the future.

2. Think about a period of history that interests you. What would it be like to live in that time? Write a few journal entries as someone living in that time

period. Think about who your character is and how they try to find meaning in the world. What is their "American Dream" and how do they try to achieve it?

3. In an interview with Popular Contemporary Writers, Octavia Butler defined science fiction by saying, "It doesn't really mean anything at all, except that if you use science, you should use it correctly, and if you use your imagination to extend it beyond what we already know, you should do that intelligently. Some [science fiction writers] look for technological solutions and others disparage technological solutions. Some write about the problems that I write about, and others write about other problems. Some think the world will go to hell and others think it will turn into ice cream. You have the same wide variety in science fiction that you have any place."

Use your imagination to picture a future reality. Write a few journal entries set in your future about someone experiencing or trying to solve a problem that matters to you.

Zion Angelo Williams Flores

Zion Flores was born June 18, 2002 and raised in Arizona. He moved to California when he was 10 and moved to Austin about a few years ago. This is only his third time really writing poetry. He found Barrio Writers through his older brother, Alberto, and has been coming ever since.

CHRIST!

1) We aren't going to point a cross at you and scream "REPENT!" or chant "Turn or burn!" at you.
2) Just because a few bad priests exist doesn't mean they're all pedophiles, right?
3) If we ask to pray with you, just do it, do you know how scary/embarrassing that can be, do you think we just love preaching to strangers on the street, we don't know how'll you'll react! You could be a murderer!
4) Don't guess, do I look like a Mormon?
5) Read a book please. Christmas is not about a fat white man Coca-Cola made, we don't give up chocolate for fun, we're not monsters, and Easter is not about a fucking rabbit!
6) Most of us are willing to talk about why we believe the things we do, so don't be afraid to ask.
7) My church family is just that, my second family, we look out for each other.
8) Christianity is built on love, the love of Jesus, our love for Jesus, our love for each other. Don't make it weird.
9) We don't hate you, we… I love you
10) So a quick recap yes some of us are horrible people but most of are great, I mean just look at me… be nice, we enjoy not being murdered, we love, I love you.
11) Thank you.

Writing Activity

1. A misconception is an incorrect view that is based on faulty thinking or understanding. What misconceptions have people made about you? How did they make you feel? How do you fight misconceptions? Write a poem or a prose piece confronting people who have judged you wrongly.

2. Zion called his church family his second family. In what ways is your life filled with different families? What makes a family? How do you define one?

3. Lists serve many purposes. Making lists is a good way of keeping track of patterns. Zion chose to write a list of things to say to people with misconceptions about his religious community. Write a story, essay, or poem that's structured in the format of a list.

Alexis Martinez

Alexis Martinez is fresh from high school and working towards her passion career as a comic artist/author. For Alexis, writing has been a way of self-expression in frustrating times. Art and writing have become the skills she hopes to excel at while graphic novels with sci-fi/fantasy elements have become a source of inspiration. Alexis says that indie films, such as Attack the Block, have inspired her art work and writing. Her script work has room for improvement, but she's only beginning.

Try

My need
To be better than the me
From before is obsessive.
I think about it every night,
Every hour, every minute, every second
Trying to be
Good
Trying to be
Amazing
Trying to be
Perfect
Yet every compliment
I get, I can't believe it

Artistic

As an artist,
I value myself
Upon how good I
Am at it.
You aren't supposed to,
Because you're special
And no matter what
You're still so valuable and good
But I don't let myself do that.
Art is what I want my life to be about,
If I'm not good I need to get better
I don't call myself a writer, because
I'll hold high standards,

I'll get depressed when
I don't think it's good.
I won't show it if I don't think it's good
I won't let myself be happy with it
I won't enjoy writing often
I have struggled as an artist,
Because I know I can do better,
And I know I'm getting better,
But it's slow

Writing Activity

1. As writers, we express our worries with words. For Alexis, she worries about trying and never being good enough, as expressed in her poem "Trying." What is something you worry about? Write out a few ideas; then use this to inspire a poem about what you worry about. Use your voice to express yourself and tackle this idea head on.

Cesar Lopez

Cesar Lopez is currently a fifteen-year-old student that goes to Santa Ana Valley High School. He is the middle child of three siblings. When he grows up, he wants to become a computer software engineer so that he can help the world advance in technology.

Untitled

Games are fun to play
Like survival games because
You always have that instinct
To survive

You never know who will challenge you
And if they do while you are in combat
You feel the adrenaline rush through your veins
Especially when you have the fear of loosing

Never will the game be boring…

Writing Activity

1. Sometimes writers use metaphors to describe or compare situations. A metaphor is a figure of speech that describes an object or action in a way that isn't literally true, but helps explain an idea or make a comparison. In a way, Cesar's poem can be interpreted as a metaphor for life. Discuss how life can be like a game.

2. What other metaphors can be used to describe life or current problems in society? Try using a metaphor for something you are strongly against (i.e. racism, homelessness, police brutality) or just a particular life experience.

Alyssa Becnel

Alyssa Gabrielle Becnel, born June 12, 2002, is an aspiring author from Nacogdoches, Texas. She has desired to be an author since the age of four, drawing inspiration from popular children's authors such as J. K. Rowling and Rick Riordan. Her views on social issues are very strong and often influence her work.

The Danger of Generalization

Frogface. Creamed spinach. Putrid ooze. Barbara was no stranger to the many insults thrown her way. Of course, she supposed she should consider herself lucky she wasn't born a few centuries earlier – back then, creatures like her were burned at the stake. But as she stood in front of the mirror and looked at her green skin and long, warty nose, she couldn't help but feel she'd gotten a bad deal.

It wasn't fair. So there was that thing with the red shoes, and then the candy house, and yeah, okay, maybe a few more princes than necessary had been turned into frogs. But then there were the fairies who tricked people into falling off cliffs. The kings who let their people starve to keep their riches. And the insurance fraud rate among certain little girls in certain red hoods had skyrocketed in the past decade. Yet somehow, only witches got a bad rap.

Barbara's mother had tried before to explain that while not all creatures were so prejudiced, Barbara must be careful. Because enough did. Why else would the rate of witch hangings be higher than that of any other species, despite the rate of high-grade crime being far lower than that of pixies or nymphs?

However, Barbara was determined to succeed and break the stereotypes that all witches were worthless, cruel, and easily outwitted. She practiced spells and hexes for an hour every night. She brewed potions better than that of her mother. She had the highest incantation success rate of anyone else in her class. And she strove to be kind as possible, even when her peers weren't kind in return. She was the perfect example of a creature, but others judged her only by what they could see.

When Barbara was accepted into Newttongue, one of the kingdom's most prestigious schools, the general uproar in her village was astounding. It wasn't such a shock when shapeshifters or sorcerers were accepted. Barbara had the credentials. She deserved to be there. Everyone knew it was only a surprise because she had broken the stereotype of "dumb witch."

Unfortunately, the stigma didn't end with Barbara's acceptance. The preconceived notions of witches were already far too ingrained into the population's mindsets to allow for individuality amongst them, all due to actions by a select few of the group. Never mind the equally as bad actions committed by other classes of creatures, or the bias of the judicial system against witches that led to a higher conviction rate, or the general pressure on witches to behave as everyone expected them to, or the fact that most turned to illegal forms of making money because other creatures didn't want to hire witches.

But this tale, so familiar to those of today, need not end in misery.

Change is possible. Through education, self-evaluation, and empowerment for those who are marginalized, together we can work towards a better tomorrow. If a friend says something bigoted, ask them to explain why they feel that way, and tell them why generalizing is harmful. If you catch yourself thinking something dismissive about those who are undervalued, stop and explore why you think that way and what you can do to change. If you see someone less privileged than you struggling, join or start an organization to help provide them with the aid they might need. All you need to do is take the time to care. Care about your fellow human beings, care about the future, care about those who aren't typically cared about.

We are all human. We all deserve the same opportunities and to be treated with the same amount of respect. Get out there and work towards making it happen.

Writing Activity

1. "The Danger of Generalization" could be considered a contemporary fable. A fable is a short story that teaches some kind of lesson or contains a moral that readers should learn from. What is the take-away lesson of Alyssa's piece? What are we supposed to learn from reading Barbara's story?

What is a lesson that is important enough to you to write about? What is a life lesson you feel passionately about? Try writing a short fable that uses creative writing to teach a lesson to readers.

3. This piece is primarily about the danger of stereotypes. A stereotype is a commonly believed idea about a particular type of person or thing that is not necessarily true or is oversimplified. What kinds of stereotypes do people attach to you? What kinds of stereotypes do you attach to other people? Do you agree that stereotypes or, as the title of this piece suggests, "generalizations" are harmful? Why or how?

Try writing a poem, short story, or first-person essay about a personal experience with stereotypes.

Amy Arelly O.

Amy Arelly O. was born August 30, 2002 in Sana Ana, California. She was raised by her hardworking mother. She is also a sister to two caring brothers. She attends Santa Ana Valley High School with dreams of going to college. She also enjoys spending time with her family and friends.

Memories Once Lost

The girl has lost many things
Shoes
Notebooks
Loved ones

Yet nothing was really lost
Just forgotten

She had given up
She had lost her memory
But one day the sun did rise

The sunshine led the way

The shoelace started to knot itself
She took her first step

The wind shared its secrets
She wrote down their stories

She danced with the flowers
And sang with the birds

She was full of affection
Like never before
And knew never again
Would she be left alone

Reflection

You look me in the eye
Disappointment is all I see

You throw insults
Point out my flaws

Every day you come back
Never the same
You went from blond to brunette
But that doesn't change
The rage you hold for me

Anger in every sentence
You throw at me
Poking at my insecurities
Funny it always
Ends the same
RED EYES
On the verge of tears

Well I'm not mad
Nor hold a grudge
I'd only hope one day
You come to see
The beautiful person
Standing before me
Because I'm only a mirror
A near image reflecting the person
Standing here

Writing Activity

1. In both pieces it seems the writer is reflecting on her personal life and perception of her self. In Barrio Writers we do not have rules, but we do have guidelines, we do not ask the writer if their work is true or about them, we ask "What inspired you to write this piece?" or "What message do you want your reader to walk away with this piece?" Now, think about those two questions, what could possibly inspire the writer to write these two pieces? What message did you receive from these poems?

2. In the poem titled "Reflection," the writer alludes that she is staring at herself in the mirror. How would you describe yourself? Try writing a poem describing what you see in a reflection—maybe focus on what is behind you or on the details of your iris or freckles. Also use details only you recognize and not so apparent to everyone who sees you.

Stephanie Gomez

Stephanie Gomez is currently a student in Connections Academy at Houston. She is a driven, young lady who loves to read and write. Stephanie is involved with the National Hispanic Institute in Houston and the National High School Scholars. She is also part of Missouri City's Youth Council. She is a passionate Latina who loves to give back to her community. She wants to pursue a high degree education and become a lawyer.

The Metal Chains

The metal chains,
cold and dark.
Getting tighter, every second
blocking the blood flow in my veins.
My past holding hands with my future.
The mask I created, snatched off my face.
I was I the front now I'm in the shadow.

The metal chain,
following me as the shadow of "Thee."
Round and round,
they take me away.
Not busy to be tamed,
so they call my name.

The metal chains,
getting tighter, every second.
Until you realize to get the key,
and break free.
Running my feet through the grassy fields
screaming
I'M FREE.

Poetry

I can't tell you my name
or my life.
All I can tell you is how
I found poetry in my life.
I love poetry.

I write from my heart
and it will stay in my heart forever.
I do not like people reading my poetry
but I can tell you how I started in 7th grade.
I fell in love with singing.
I would make up rhymes,
and it felt like I was making poetry.
My friend helped me make them.
They are supportive to me.
I love them.
If it was not for them,
I would not love.
Poetry.
That is how I fell in love with poetry
and now it is in my life.

Writing Activity

1. Stephanie's poem 'The Metal Chains' explores the relation between the speaker and "metal chains." What do the chains symbolize, or what do the chains mean to this person's life? Write a poem where you explore the relationship between a person and an object. What would the object symbolize in the person's life?

2. What is your favorite thing? Write a poem about how you came to discover it and how it influences you now.

Christian Sida

Christian Sida was born on January 15, 1999. He was born shy and very quiet. At the age of 4, he met his future best friend, Jose-Emanuel Rosales. It wasn't until middle school that he started to be more outgoing. In 8th grade, he joined a dance class. At first, he thought about leaving until he said "Ehh" and decided to stay. Starting high school freshman year, he took another dance class and decided that this was his passion apart from music making itself. In March of his junior year, he was notified of his best friend's death. He committed suicide. After this tragic event, he decided to continue with his passion for dance. After graduating high school, he will be attending Santa Ana College in August and will be studying for a masters in Mathematics and Dance.

Identity

Dear BLANK

I don't have an identity. Because having an identity is too boring. Sure, my name is Christian Alonzo Sida. Sida, I never knew the meaning of that word or what it meant to me until I met the Sidas. Sure it's fun being a Sida but that's not me. I just don't want to be known as Christian Alonzo Sida or CAS for short. I want to be known as a dancer, an artist, a music enthusiast, a beatboxer, a comedian, a friend, a best friend. Scribble Scribble Scribble, Blanks Blanks and more Blanks. You see I lied, I do want to be known as CAS, but also as a dancer, an artist, a comedian a... You get the point. So I guess I do have an identity, and it's not so boring after all. I guess that's it. I will be, and forever will be known as CAS, Christian Alonzo Sida, the dancer, the artist… BLAH BLAH BLAH Scribble Scribble Scribble....

Sincerely,
CAS
P.S. Saying my name is too long.

Lucid

"It is as if a force, external, has given me my dream house. This particular house was different, very organized. I knew where everything was. It was pretty huge. The house sat on the corner of La Verne. It was surrounded by a black gate in which the front part would slide open. Walking into my new home was surreal. The living room was pretty huge, huge enough to throw a party. Maybe I should invite the guys later. Anyways, to the left of the living room was my comics room. As soon as you walk in, an array of colorful posters and images fill your iris. On the center wall I have a 6-foot poster of Captain America and The Flash, side by side. Surrounding them were shelves upon shelves from "Spectacular Spiderman #1" to "Infinity Wars." Taking stairs to the second floor, the first room, my favorite of them all, my dance room. The mirrors up front covering the whole front walls. The walls were white. Not the usual white, but brighter. The wooden floor was the same color, it felt as if there was no ground and I was just in the air, floating. It felt as if the dance room was fake, as I reach to touch the bright walls, my hand just went through."

Well I got out of bed, managing not to trip over my dirty clothes. My eyesight was still blurry. I couldn't find my glasses, until I saw the glare of the lens next to my bed.

I opened my door,
I went to the kitchen,
Grabbed the cereal,
Opened the fridge,
Grabbed the milk,
Poured a bowl,
and sat down in the living room, eating.
In my apartment.

Letter of Reassurance

Dear Emanual,

It was just a normal school day. Woke up, went to school. 3rd period came. I was sitting in my chair. I felt the vibration of the phone in my pocket. It was my mother. I looked down to see the message:

"White boy passed away today"

"Want me to pick you up?"

Look, don't get mad but I told her I didn't care. That it didn't bother me that you passed away. I didn't realize it but I was in shock. I just said it didn't bother me but it did.

As soon as I arrived from school, it kicked in. First it was anger. Anger at the world, at everyone! I blame them for what you did. For locking yourself in the bathroom, and shooting yourself in the chest. I was angry. Too angry to see straight. Thoughts kept popping into my mind.

"It was your parents fault! They didn't help you, they just shunned you out!"

I fell asleep.

I woke up, my face was tired from the sobbing earlier. I looked in the mirror to see the trails my tears left on my face.

You see, that's where I started blaming myself.

"I fucked up."

I don't know if you remember but you texted me a few days before your passing, if I wanted to hang out with you. I ignored you, I was scared because I knew you were doing things that were wrong. I didn't want to be a part of it. But in the end, it wasn't because you wanted to me to follow in your steps, but because you needed and old friend. One you grew up with since you were 4 years old.

I'm sorry I ignored you, I hope you know that if I can change the past I would. I hope you're doing well up there. We will meet soon enough my friend.

Sincerely,
Your childhood friend, Chris

Writing Activities

1. What does your name mean to you? Free write a letter to someone about the meaning of your name.

Free writing is writing continuously without stopping for a period of time. If you can't think of what to write next, just write "I can't think of what to write," or "scribble scribble, BLAH BLAH" until you think of something to write. Try setting a timer for 5-10 minutes and free write until the time runs out. Don't worry about spelling or grammar, just keep on writing down whatever comes to mind.

2. If you could have your dream house, what would it look like? Fold a paper into eight squares. In each square, draw a different view or room in your dream house. Start with a view from the outside, then draw the bedroom, the kitchen, the living room, the backyard, or any other rooms you would want. Write a story or poem that describes what it would feel like to walk around in your dream house.

3. Is there someone who left you before you had a chance to say goodbye? What would you have said to them if you had that chance? Write a letter to them describing how you felt when they left and what you wish you could have told them.

Hannah M. Abbott

Hannah Abbott was born on June 8, 2000. She is a very soft-spoken girl that loves to read, draw, and listen to music. She comes from a family of readers and even some writers. She is mainly seen as the outcast but in reality, she is the girl with a big heart who has been through a lot.

My Starry Night's Journey

As I walked along my small feet screamed for me to stop and rest. My journey has been long and treacherous; but as I came closer to my destination I became ecstatic at the thought of seeing him again. His voice strong in my head promising me we would see each other again. I kept my pace at a constant with his promise, I had to see him again. Ever since he had left, the ache of my heart grew in strength. I cried many times we never got to share; the memories missed, so I made the decision to go to him.

I've been on my journey for many years. These years have been long and tiring. Walking endlessly towards the one for whom I have so many questions: 'How are you?', 'Why did you have to go?', 'Was it my fault?' I push on with the promise of answers from the one I've been wanting so desperately to see since he had gone away. I look down at my small shoes, torn, worn out from my traveling. Sometimes I feel discouraged and wonder why I'm trying. I have discouraging questions for myself that make me want to stop, turn around and go home. Questions like: 'Does he even care?', 'Does he even remember me?', 'Does he want to see me?', 'What if he hates me?'

I push away the discouraging thoughts as I make my way up a gentle hill, lush and green even in the cover of night. I then reach the top of the hill and take in the picture before me. My breath is stolen from me as I gaze at a small town with one large castle like structure surrounded by many beautiful rolling and lush hills waving gently in the night breeze. I feel the wind kiss my cheeks as it draws my heart shaped face towards the even more stunning sky. As I look up with my hazel eyes I'm awe-struck at the sea of stars and waves of blue, black, yellow and white that fill the humongous sky. I feel the wind blow my long brown hair across my shoulders, tickling them giving me a wave of chills, that made me shiver. I wrapped my arms around my body shielding it from the chilly night's breeze. I look back up at the sky and marvel at the moon, giant, in the sky; but soon I reminded myself of the journey I'm so close to finishing. I then slowly tear my gaze away from the sky and make my way towards the small town surrounding the castle like structure.

While heading to the small town I begin to rehearse what I would say when he opens the door. 'Hello, how are you?', 'Hey it's me.' All the starting sentences that ran through my mind sounded as strange as eating French fries and vanilla ice cream together. I guess I'll figure it out when it comes down to it. I soon reached the edge of the small, dimly lit town. My heart began to race as I made my way to his home. 'I'm really here, finally after so many years,' I thought. I reached into my small jeans pocket and pulled out a folded piece of paper. I had written his address down before starting this journey so I wouldn't have to search through the town embarrassing myself with each failed attempt, I unfolded the paper and stared at the address; 4392 Jackson street. I looked around me to at least get an estimate of where I was. I finally found the small sign that said 'Jackson Street'. I was already there, my heart pounded in my chest. I began to walk and count the homes' numbers as I made my way to him.

My breath began to get shorter as I got closer, 4387, 4388, 4389 ... I couldn't help but stop and take a breath. If I had shown up at his home hyperventilating I don't think that would be a good thing. I then looked up slowly towards the sky to calm my anxious nerves with its beauty. I've never known why but I've always found comfort in the night. Ever since I was a little girl. I stared again awestruck and amazingly calmed instantaneously. I decided it was time to keep moving. I started to walk again counting down to him. 4390, 4391, 4392. I have arrived, finally, after so many years of traveling I was going to see him again. I stood in front of the small cottage with the mahogany door. I felt the blood rush to my head and from my limbs as I tried to make my move to knock on the beautiful door. Finally, after a few seconds I took a deep breath and raised a shaking fist to knock on the heavy door. 'Knock, Knock, knock' was heard on the door. A few seconds, which felt like millenniums, later a familiar and very much missed man answered the door. With teary eyes I said, "Hey Dad." And as I closed them to blink away tears I was quickly embraced with strong and warm arms.

Writing Activity

1. Is there something you've dreamed about doing for a long time, or someone you've dreamed about meeting? Take a few minutes to imagine what it would feel like to do that thing or meet that person. Close your eyes and imagine what that scene would look like, smell like, or sound like. Now get out your paper and start describing the event, place, or meeting.

2. Go back and re-read the piece and look at how Hannah builds anticipation. What does she do to make you feel like the event or meeting is getting closer? Now go back and look at the notes you just took and think about how you can build anticipation in your piece. Try to make the reader feel like they are with you as you anticipate the event or meeting.

Cameron Daniels

Hello, my name is Cameron Daniels, and I am 14 years old. I am a 10th grader at Nacogdoches High School where I hope to graduate and then pursue my dream of becoming a doctor. I am very active at my church and sing in two community choirs. For my work in singing and theatre, I've received two awards from the Nacogdoches Board of Trustees (2014and 2015). I hope that as you read both of my pieces, you connect with them and they, in some way, help you.

How it Feels to Be Me in the United States

It feels like all hope is lost for the United States to me.

To be me in the United States is to be a person who is scared to walk past a police officer thinking is today going to be my last day

To be me in the United States is to be a person whose parents won't let you go anywhere because "I don't know them." Or "It's not safe." "How do you know it's not safe?" And "You don't know them because you don't go to school with them." I reply back, but it's all for nothing. I still know the answer will be no. Sad and Depressed I return to my room.

To be me in the United States is to be a person who makes friends you think will have your back but yet stabs you in it.

But to be me in the United States is to be a person who can rise above the stereotypes which makes my victory even more glorious.

To be me in the United States is to be a person who knows what type of friends he wants thanks to his mistakes and doesn't waste time on fake and phony people.

To be me in the United States is to be a person who stands up and fights for what he believes in.

Yes, my life may not be the best but it makes me try harder and pushes me to overcome and learn each and every day.

Stereotypes

The list of stereotypes goes on and on for African Americans.

From always eating
Chicken
Greens
Peas
And Cornbread
To

Living in the ghetto
Cussing
And fighting

Most of these stereotypes aren't true. I don't live in the ghetto and eat greens cabbages peas and cornbread. People today kill me with that just because I'm black doesn't mean I quote on quote act black. People judge me daily wondering if I'm going to steal from or fight them. Me personally, I wouldn't do that because I know my parents would kill me if I ever did that. Most people don't get to know me because they are afraid of my skin color. If people would get to know me for me, we would probably would be friends. But that's stereotypes for you they don't treat you well They put you in this bind that's hard to get out of. The stereotypes of this kind make me so mad because a lot of people use stereotypes of race and gender to categorize people they don't even know. The world would be a better place if we could all get along and not identify people by their race or the stereotypes they hear but by their personality and common interest. But the way the U.S. is looking today it will be a long time before that dream will happen.

Writing Activity

1. In Cameron's piece "How it Feels to be Me in the United States," he writes powerfully about the contrast between how others feel about him and how he feels about himself. The piece talks about how he wants to change his world and how he wants to respond to the things people think about him. Do you feel similarly to Cameron, or does it feel really different to be you in the United States? Try your hand at writing a "How it Feels to be Me in the United States" poem.

2. After reading "Stereotypes," get out a piece of paper and make your own list of stereotypes that people might apply to you and then write a response piece to the list. Try to include a range of types of words: adjectives, verbs, and nouns.

Cristian Dominguez

Hi! Do you know Dory's lost brother Cristian Dominguez? He's been lost for 14 years. He's been lost to writing and books. It's been 14 years that any of us have seen him. He was born and raised in Austin, TX, having Dory and 6 other siblings. Cristian is here, but can you really do me a favor? Put Cristian back at the aquarium. In the near future, Cristian would attend St. Stephens' aquarium, and in the future, he would like to attend, for his college life, UT McComb School's aquarium and Harvard's aquarium. Cristian has been working hard. In November, he received a letter from United Way Austin's CEO thanking him for his hard work helping them for 2 years, making him family. He also received a message the day before his birthday from former president Barack Obama. Please vote for Cristian when he runs for president in 2036. He will be the first fish president!

Our Chicano Movements

I am part of the Chicano community. We aren't 'bout that thug life, nun 'bout that shit. Working hard for our parents is our thing. You can't blame us for anything.

Trying to make it alive is also our thing. Not even Geico could save us 15%! Trying to make it alive, yo, you get it.

We aren't 'bout that thug life, nun 'bout that shit. We trying to make those A+, but trying to have fun.

You won't roast us any better, we were roasted in our childhood. Mexicans moms would tell us, "¡Ya ves! ¡Por pendejo!" Don't you worry; she won't use that chancla like she used it on us.

We aren't 'bout that thug life, but neither is State Farm.

You better eat your taco de pastor before we get mad. ¡Y, no, no sabemos el español!

Remember to reserve 40 tickets for us! All our tíos, tías, hermanas, hermanos, abuelo, abuela, mama, papa, primos y primas would be there!

Luego, no chinges, don't you cry. We aren't 'bout that sad life porque luego vamos a tener una pinche problema. We are supposed to work hard if not nosotros son chingados con el pinche palo.

Y todavia, you can still have all those Mexicans memes stored up on your phone to try to use it against us. It won't be any better, we were roasted before. Our moms would usually say el Cucuy viene a la cocina en la noche. Don't be dumb, don't jump or anything. She will tell you, "¿Hijo de tu pinche madre, vives en la calles? ¡No más quieres tragar!" We can even roast your ass if you insist.

We aren't the only ones wanting to eat taco de pastor. Our moms would go to Zumba, and say they are on a "diet." A few hours later, they are caught ordering 5 tacos de pastor!

But we are a very welcoming community! If you ever really want to join, you will have to go through multiple tests to see if you can be with us! Just be warned, you will be roasted, but roasted until your ass burns.

We will give you the carne asada, just don't tell our moms and dads! They will be mad at us because they spend their money on expensive food. We are here for everybody, just trying to make it alive nowadays!

They Say, I Say

They say I am Indian by my skin color.
I say to them I am a Caucasian. I am brown and white. White by my ancestors, brown by my ancestors.

They say I am weak by my looks.
I say I am powerful as a bald eagle fighting back at other bald eagles.

They say I am a nerd because I am good at reading and social studies.
I say I am who I want to be.

They say Pokémon is for little kids due to Pokémon cards.
I say I am Pokémon 679, a Kalos natural Pokémon.

They say I am not a fighter.
I say I fight back as if I was a parrot who can fight back by words, and yes I know how to fight.

They say I don't forget things easily.
I say I am related to Dory. Bitch, do you even know me?

They said I am into Bernie Sanders because I love his viewpoints.
I say FEEL THE BERN BITCHES! Read the news and watch it as if you were a fucking dumb mummy!

They say I am too old because I am mature.
I say yes, thank you, at least I am not you.

They say I am good enough to make perfect A's and B's.
I say, bitch thank you, but no thanks. You can always treat me as if I was that fucking nerdy worm. I can always treat you like a total douche bag!

In What I Believe

I believe in fair equal rights. I believe in women and men equally. I believe in people that are Christian, Atheist, and Muslim equally. I believe in straight, gays, lesbians, bisexuals, and transgender equally. I believe in liberals, socialists, and conservatives equally. I believe in Democrats, Republicans, Libertarians, and Greens equally. I believe in whites, blacks, browns, yellows, oranges, reds and even blues as Smurfs equally. I believe in women who have and have not gotten an abortion equally. I believe in El Chapo equally. I believe people can do all the fuck they want.

BUT WHAT I DO NOT BELIEVE IN is people stereotyping others. BUT WHAT I DO NOT BELIEVE IN is people stereotyping others. BUT WHAT I DO NOT BELIEVE IN is people being ignorant as hell. BUT WHAT I DO NOT BELIEVE IN is people running our society who aren't capable of doing so. No fucking law degree? BYE BITCH! BUT WHAT I DO NOT BELIEVE IN is people who act like they are above the law.

Writing Activity

1. What are the core values and beliefs that drive and motivate you? Write a manifesto declaring those values and beliefs.

2. Write about a time when you stood up for your rights or the rights of another. What did you say or do? How did you make your voice heard?

3. How would you describe your community? Your community could include your city, neighborhood, family, friends, church, or school. You may choose to write an ode poem celebrating your community.

Patricia Limon

Patricia Naomi Limon is a 15 year old who lives in Santa Ana, California. She is in love with music and psychology. She hopes to enter the psychology field in the future to help others. She adores her entire family which consists of her mother, grandmother, and three sisters in which she is the second oldest. She has high hopes for the world's future and her own as well.

What's Wrong

I no longer ask where or why we went wrong.
All I know is that we are what went wrong.

What's wrong?

We slash others wings because we cannot reach their altitudes
We kill others for being different,
As if they were the true villains

What's wrong?

We ostracize people whose ancestors went through agony because of yours
We teach children to loathe themselves because of what they look like
The worst of it all?
Villains never change
The ones we love we estrange.
Why?
Emma fell in love with Mia
Bobby knew he was meant to be a Sofia

Like others before me,
I fight for a better tomorrow,
A better place.

Until then the thick blanket of darkness that suffocates me and the monsters that lurk within it keep me wide awake.

Writing Activity

1. Do you believe media headlines either through newspapers or social media (FB, Twitter, Instagram) effect our day? How so? How can we alter how we react or interact with such news?

2. What are some of themes the poem speaks to? How are these themes part of current media headlines? Write a response piece: What advice or what positive outlook would you provide to someone who shares the feelings and opinions in this poem. Be creative—write a letter, a response poem or just a "feel good" story addressing these themes.

Giselle Godinez

Giselle Godinez is 14 years old and the youngest in her family. She was born and raised in the city of Santa Ana, soon to be attending Valley High school. This is her second year in Barrio Writers. Giselle enjoys cross country, listening to One Direction, and reading books. She hopes to study hard and get accepted to an Ivy League school of her choice.

Dear Batman

Dear Batman,

I don't know where to start but I know it'll never end. The reasons I love you so much it hurts me. Lourdes, that beautiful name. Unique. Just like you. I know that at least once during fourth period on class, while we're talking and playing around instead of doing our work, you demand to be called Batman. Then I would call myself Deadpool.

Every morning, round and round, like a carousal. Never getting sick and tired of it all. I figured we would be friends when I noticed you had a pencil bag with Harry Potter on it. I just didn't see how close we would soon become once fuckboys were right down our alley. His name I wont say because the thought of it just makes me want to throw up but he will be called "Big Nose." He used you, lied to you, betrayed you, and never apologized. I see how some people would say that it's stupid so say you are in love especially when you are so young but it's only said because they, themselves didn't have that feeling. I was there for you and vice versa. It took you a few months to ease some of the pain. As bad as this sounds it was all thrown away when you found another buttface. He was worse than Big Nose including the fact that buttface had a bigger nose than the first jackass.

I saw the effect it had on you once your honeymoon phase was over. It turned on waterfalls in your eyes. During those days of sadness there were days of smiles and laughter where we both forgot our sorrow. Those days of story-telling with sick and twisted endings for the bad guys. Those days of fangirling over Shawn Mendes or One Direction. Those days of bringing snacks to social studies expecting everyone around us to comment on how much food we bring. Those days were what we lived for. I remember you asked me once to describe you in one word and I said "nothing." The word nothing. You looked so disappointed. I then explained to you why I said nothing. There are no words in the dictionary are enough to describe the amazing human being that is you. I'd also say thank you right now in a very random place because why not? The thing is I've never felt like I've thanked you enough or properly. You've just done so much for me. Including outing me out to boys I like but I will scold you about it later. See, this is why I'm bad at thanking people. I get side tracked. Like Thomas and Friends when Thomas was going too fast and decided to go off course to get his delivery done but the non-cartoon version that's super creepy because they are always smiling like pedophiles. Damn it, I'm getting off track again.

Anyway, thank you. You've made my day a little bit brighter and a lot more exciting. This is still a bad "thank you" but hey, it's getting published. One thing I wont say thank you for is not stopping me from drinking coffee. Coffee is evil towards me. The one day I should have drank coffee during Open House at school when we did that project on Gentrification. I felt the need to make everyone proud us and I was nervous. Especially Sarah, because she was aware of the project and I had learned about it in Barrio Writers. Buttface, aka, Jorge still fancied you and treated you somewhat right but we never liked each other, as you well know. He was and still is an asshole, can you blame me? Open House with him around wasn't the best but I was with you so I coped.

I don't really know where I'm going with this. I guess I just really, deep down, wanted to comment on how much of a dickwad he was.

This past year was sucky. One of the only highlights of this year was six days before the end of the school year. On a Thursday, one day before the last school dance, it was after you two finally broke it off and only some people were still buzzing about it, he said something. So I said something. He threw a water bottle at me. So I punched him in the face. I don't know what was going on in my mind. It happened in a flash. Once that water bottle hit my stomach, it hit me. Pun not intended. He did so many things to you that I'm too lazy to type them all. He deserves a small taste of what he's done. You know from my past messages that I've wanted to hit him or throw that stupid basketball at his big head that he always held onto from the moment he said you were stupid.

It pretty much triggered me. It triggered me to go up to him, stop the fight you two were having about him hitting me, and threw the punch. He looked shocked. He thought I was all talk and no action. So did the small group that was already surrounding us, getting bigger by the second as they caught a glimpse of my fist colliding with his face. Ugly face, I might add. He screamed at me, tried to hit me too but was held back by the crowd that was surprisingly not filled with school staff. I ignored all of this and instead paid attention to the steady flow of blood leaving his mouth. Everything that has been building up, whether it be what past things he's don't or any of my problems, I let out. I wanted more.

Is that bad? I wanted to keep punching until someone was able to stop me. I walked away once the scene was over and you had left with the most stunned and speechless expression. Even after being shunned, threatened, and hated on by the people we called our friends, we kept our heads held high. I am very proud of us. Of course when we went to the school office and gave our statement because someone from the inside told us buttface had tattle-taled. He never mentioned to his parents that he initiated the so-called "fight" which was a bit hilarious to me because he wanted to make himself a victim to my bullying. In the end the pathetic apology we all had to make was stupid. I only humor in it when it was my turn to apologize to buttface and tried to hold in my laughter when I mentioned punching him and then that making him cry. The school needs to fire and put together a new school staff because I know how unsafe it made you feel when Danny's girlfriend threatened to punch us if we ever came near buttface or his friends. I would definitely go for a fight if it didn't affect my record. Thankfully school was over and our trip to New York and Boston was our next stop.

I will be completely honest and say NYC/Boston was the most exciting and amazing experience of my short, fourteen-year-old life. Sometimes I didn't show it because I was so damn tired. I haven't seen you since. I want to see you but you're too busy and sadly it isn't working out for me since I have no life. Either way, alone you are Batman, I am Deadpool. Together we are Batpool. Forever and always.

Sincerely,
that girl who wrote you a fanfiction.

¿Me Quieres?

Mi madre me dijo ke trabaje
Mi papa me dijo ke siempre voy a ser su princesa
Mi ermana me dijo ke corra para ke baje de peso
Mi mejor amiga me dice sus secretos, no todos
Mi, pero se me keda mirando como si estoy loca cuando bailo sin importancia
Mi tía me dice de su casa fabulosa y su hija "perfecta"
Mis maestros me dicen ke tengo un bueno cerebro
Nadien me dice ke me quieren

Home

Ice cold hands causing "accidents"
Taking us away
Do we stand a chance of living
The only thing on my mind
Take me home
Oh how I wish I could see my mom
Heart in my throat
You're not a friend
Take me home

I've hardly slept
Since…I don't know how long or when
Don't know where I am
Missing my bestfriend
Haven't seen the light
Only a black bag
"Take me home" are the words I think but never speak
I hear voices saying "cayate carbón" every time there are cries of a boy or girl pleading for mercy
I hear the cries and the silence afterwards
Take me home

I used to be so happy
I now have the feeling of something ending
Taking me out of the darkness
I come to face a mask
Cowards, I think
As I close my eyes I utter the words
The three most important words to me
"Take me home," I whisper
And I am gone
With just one breath leaving my chapped lips

7-year-old me

Dear younger self,

Get used to running because your older self stupidly agreed to join cross country. I mean…it's not bad but it'll give future you a little boost, you get me? Don't grow up yet because mom will start giving you responsibilities. We don't want that. Spend some time with Peter Pan. If you're still a fan of puffy, neon, pink skirts, enjoy it because periods suck plus I only own jeans and a few shorts. Don't be annoying and eat healthier. Don't go buying 10 bags of Cheetos at la trokita in front of the apartment building just because Beida does it too. Resist! You will thank me later. Don't get into fights because believe me, you'll give the best punch of your life to a boy at the end of eighth grade. Keep making your siblings proud. Most importantly, keep checking out fourteen books from the library and writing a lot. You'll get better.

Sincerely,
You

(p.s. you're still going to be a hardcore fan of one direction, it's not a phase)

EXPOSED

Hello, Villa. You will be exposed.
Your school staff is bullshit.
Just a warning
Shout out to Mrs. Gumuzo

Writing Activity

1. Think of someone in your life that has been through important experiences with you. What moments stand out in your mind as moments that defined your relationship or a point of growth you went through together? Write a letter to that person about the meaningful moments you shared together.

2. In "¿Me Quieres?" Giselle writes in Spanish with phonetic spelling. Phonetic spelling is writing words using a system of spelling that expresses the pronunciation of words rather than the traditional spelling. What do you think about the effect that phonetic spelling creates? How does phonetic spelling affect the message or meaning of the poem? Try writing a poem using phonetic spelling that expresses the ways you pronounce words.

3. If you could share a message with your younger self, what would you say? Would you give some advice about how to live your life? Would you warn yourself about something? Would you encourage yourself to keep on being the same? Write a letter to your younger self with a message about living in the future.

Adrian Martinez

Adrian Martinez is a 14-year-old sophomore at Orange County School of the Arts. He has been living in Santa Ana since birth with his mom and dad, along with two little sisters and an adorable dog. Adrian loves to play his favorite songs on guitar and loves listening to KoRn, Slipknot, and Pantera. He has a craving for Takis. He hopes to attend UCI and get a new electric guitar… before then.

Extrovert

WHY DO YOU DO THIS TO ME?!?! I'm the strongest force!!! and YOU know it!!!

You choose not to show me to the world. Yes, I know that you don't give a crap about what other people say but, you still choose not to show me. Come on I'm the best spirit to give you the ride of your life. Why did Slipknot have to give you an idea of creating me?!?! What was the point of creating me?!?! If I'm not being introduced to the outside while I support you on the inside. I know I snap sometimes but I like the outside. Look I want to help you by showing the world that your coming. I just hope one day you choose me to take over…………………………

Writing Activity

1. Do you know the difference between "introvert" and "extrovert"? Discuss as a group, then let everyone know which term you identify with the most.

2. Read "An Introvert's Open Letter to Extroverts: 5 Things You Should Know About Me" in the Huffington Post (www.huffingtonpost.com/tree-franklyn/an-introverts-open-letter_b_6157998.html). Write your own letter from your perspective—maybe focus on a teen's perspective versus a general letter.

Jackie Ramirez

She was born May 27, 2003 in Texas. She was raised by her mom, step-dad, and grandparents, who all played a huge role in her life. Along with them, she has 2 younger brothers, one the age of 8 and the other 5 months. Jackie also has 2 years of experience in volleyball and track and is hoping to continue that in high school. She will be an incoming freshman at Nacogdoches High School. She plans on going to college, attending med school, and becoming a surgeon, which she will be willing to work for just like her family has taught her to do, along with many great things.

The Moment

As I roam the halls, I am visible but not heard
As I sit in class I am smart, but not enough
In a friendship I'm nice, but not enough
When I'm on that track I'm skilled, Indeed I am enough
What's it like to not be heard?
Simple as it is
It's as if you're not enough
It's as if no one is interested enough
To hear the words coming from your mouth
Until it is no longer a necessity to be heard
Why you may ask?
Why is it no longer a necessity to be heard
Once I step foot on that track?
Well simple as it is
It's the great feeling you get as your running
The feeling that says not everyone can do
Exactly what I'm doing now
Not everyone has put exactly
As much dedication as I have
So as simple as it is
As you're in pain, you feel something growing inside
Something that is not disappointing
Something that is not meant to be taken for granted
Something that will not disappear soon
It is a feeling most people develop
By changing their appearance
To make themselves feel worthy
Well simple as it is
This feeling that people go crazy about is called
Confidence

Writing Activity

1. Write a poem, song, rap, or narrative about a time when you felt invisible in a crowd. What did it feel like, why did you feel that way, and what did you do?

2. Write about ways that you love yourself. What are some things you do to improve your self-confidence and inspire you to push through hard things you experience? Why is it important to practice self-care and take time to make sure you are taking care of you?

Rafael Flores

Rafael Flores was born on May 4, 2004. He likes the Mexico's soccer team, cares about his family and loves (wait for it)… spicy food!!!!!!!!!!!!!!!!!!!!!!!!!

Looking for freedom

Is like looking for your family
but you're an orphan and your
family was shot to death by
the local gang

Freedom is a cloud in the
wind and rich people in there
planes but you're a poor kid that
eats trash for dinner

Darkness

Is a terrible place
you are alone
scared of what will happen
to you, at this point you are
going to want to die

But out of nowhere a small
light show at the tip of the
horrors and a spark of hope
shines off the fear on your
soul and human flesh

Happiness takes over your
mind as if it was a drug
The cold water in the river
feel nice as it passes your
toes that makes feel at home
The wind blows your face as if
you are flying with the birds

You think, "Nothing can go wrong."
But you spoke too soon and at end

of the mountains you see a wave
of darkness coming your way!!!!!!!
But it is too late………

Darkness came back to its kingdom
and his throne as the king of the land!
You know what is coming so you get ready
and this time you are willing to die for the
Land you call home

The last goodbye

You are going camping
with your family today!
Sadly your grandma and
cousin are staying back
"That's okay," you think

But it wasn't okay
because that is the last
time you will see her alive
You didn't know that she
stopped going to the doctor
or taking her meds or that
she just gave up……….

She didn't tell anyone but
my mother and I bet that
was killing my mom to
know that she was going
to die

You see, she was doing
fine in my eyes and she
looked like she was going
to stay with us but I was
wrong…………………..

My last words to my grandma
was, "god bless you grandma."

Writing Activity

1. If you could say something to someone you care about right now, what would you say? Write a poem where you say everything you've ever wanted to someone that you haven't gotten a chance to say. What will you say?

2. Rafael writes a poem where he explores 'happiness' and 'darkness,' two opposing forces. Write a poem where you explore two opposing feelings in one poem.

Julia Gomez-Rangel

Julia Gomez-Rangel was born and raised in Corpus Christi, Texas. On August 16, 2017, she will finally be old enough to start learning how to drive. She aspires to do many things in life, including learning to ride a motorcycle and eventually owning her own.

No One Ever Takes Warnings Seriously (Especially When It Comes in Essay Format)

Dear Younger Self (15),

You shouldn't be reading this. Who knows what your reading of this letter will cause. I would make that issue the topic of the letter, but my last letter covered this topic extensively enough. World-changing consequences aside, it is completely unethical for me to send this letter. What have I done to deserve a chance to change what has already passed. Does anyone deserve this kind of privilege? Is it a privilege or is it a human right? We have the power, and by not allowing people to change the past we could be obstructing their right to pursue happiness. Technically time traveling to the past shouldn't be possible, but I guess if you receive this letter someone went above the speed limit of the universe. Nevertheless, here I am writing this letter knowing that I shouldn't yet be doing so.

If you received my last letter, which I hope not because I will admit that I rambled quite a bit, then you know why it is a terrible idea to communicate with your past-self. In case you didn't, the main idea was that the risk of disrupting the timeline was far too high when compared to the benefit of having a little help with any of your future obstacles. You already know this though. You're smart.

Should I regard you as a different person or younger me? Technically you're both, but I feel that talking to a person who just happens to share fifteen years of the exact same memories is simpler than constantly mixing the two of us because I refer to us as the same person. This is a philosophical question that will keep both of us up at 3:00 a.m. You're welcome.

So other than knowing you're going to live to see your twenty-fifth birthday and time travel exists you shouldn't know anything about the future. This isn't an excuse to be reckless. I didn't get to where I am by throwing myself off of cliffs and lazing about. I know you. I'm you but stronger, smarter, and with more impulse control. If I thought I was guaranteed to live to see the Earth revolve round the Sun twenty-five times I would have probably broken so many bones.

To be honest, I find it therapeutic to talk to you. It's not like writing to your future-self. I'm not stumbling over questions and sweating with uncertainty.

Last year's letter was a bit stressed for lack of a better word but it wasn't the ramblings of a person in fear but rather of a person experiencing an existential crisis. I've calmed down though, for the most part. I still have my moments when my thoughts are too loud and I sound manic but I find that I just need to focus on what's real to quiet all the questions that distract me.

This letter is longer than intended but it could be longer. Ironically, I don't have the time to delve into every thought in my head. This letter is not as fun as my last letter but telling you to hit your head again would make it seem like I have self-destructive tendencies.

Sincerely,
Your Older-Self (25)

Writing Activity

1. We, as writers, have amazing imaginations; we use that to our advantage in order to think of endless possibilities, even when it comes to thinking of possibilities for ourselves. Think about the future, whether that be five, ten, or fifteen years from now. Write a letter from that year and your future to the you of today. Beware: any secrets you share from the future will permanently disrupt the space-time continuum and change your future forever.

Cassidy Lapierre

Cassidy Lapierre is a sophomore at Texas State University where she is studying English. She is the President of Inkspot Creative Writing Club and has hopes to go to grad school for Library Science.

Diabetic Horror Stories

I'll spot something, a headphone cord poking from a pocket, no, a pump tube. I'll cross a room, the quad, a street even to start a conversation with someone like me. A fellow diabetic. Those are the times, the coveted times, we get to swap our stories and sigh. Our diabetic horror stories.

A friend that I met at diabetes camp started dating a mutual friend. I was talking to him and mentioned he should always have snacks on him in case she got low. He looked at me with such confusion that I realized she had never told him she was diabetic.

A different friend once told me that on his first date with his first girlfriend he didn't pull out his pump to take any insulin throughout the entire date. Not for dinner. Not for the popcorn at the movie. Not for the ice cream afterwards. He was almost hospitalized.

When I started marching band in high school, the directors kept an extra eye on me. On their Disney trip the previous year, a diabetic girl decided she didn't want to be diabetic on that trip so she stopped monitoring it. By the end of the week, she had to be dragged onto a helicopter to be taken to the hospital, nearing a coma with every passing minute.

There was a boy in my biology class who pointed to my pump and told me that his sister also had diabetes. She refused to count her carbs so her parents had to put locks on the cupboards to keep watch on how much she ate. She threw a massive fit, to the point of wielding her knife at her own family. Protective Services had to come and take her away.

When I was helping at a summer camp for diabetic children, there was a boy in the first-grade group who had been diagnosed less than a month before. This kid was a down right bully. He would call the other kids names and push them over. He would try to fight the nurses that were giving him insulin. He was angry. Unbelievably angry. He was one day away from becoming one of the countless diabetic horror stories. But he wasn't unreachable, not yet. He realized that I was angry too. We were all angry. But there's no one to be angry at, it's just how life turns out sometimes. He turned his anger to sports and is now one of the best runners on his cross-country team.

I see the way these able-bodied people look at us, look at me. A flash of sadness, of shock, of… disgust at something we can't control. Except… I can. No, I can't control whether or not my body produces insulin but I can control the way I think about it. I don't have to tuck my pump into my pocket or check my blood sugar in the cover of a bathroom stall. Of letting them ask questions, and giving them their answers.

It's not a lack of ability that causes our downfalls, it is an abundance of our shame. I am diabetic. I refuse to be a diabetic horror story.

Writing Activity

1. Do you have an illness and/or disability? Write an essay where you explore your illness and/or disability. How is your life different than others? What hardships do you encounter? How do people react to your illness and/or disability?

Esmeralda Zenaida Rivera

Sixteen-year-old Zenaida lives in Santa Ana and is currently entering her 3rd year at Godinez Fundamental High School. She enjoys traveling to places full of nature to capture beauty with her camera. Her hobbies are reading, discovering new music no matter the language, practicing for color guard, changing her hairstyle, editing pictures, and writing in her free time. Zenaida attends an afterschool program called Nicholas Academic Center where she has learned leadership by becoming vice president of the K-Pop Club. Every Tuesday, she spends her time in ballet where she relieves her stress from school by dancing. Zenaida has overcome many obstacles to be the person she is today. She is often told she has an old soul, which she strongly loves. Zenaida works hard to make her family proud and to hopefully become a student at Cornell University in the future.

Trail of Gains and Losses Part 1

October 23, 2000.9:31PM.

As my little brown eyes came in contact with the bright white light, they shut tightly like two venus flytraps. My heart began to rapidly slam against my chest. My lips slowly parted, allowing me to take my first breath. As I breathed and my heart pumped, I let out a cry of joy. Then another again and again and again. I was out. Out of the darkness and closed up space I had been in for months. Now I was in the arms of the owner of the cave. The owner, was a beautiful woman who now carefully held me as she smiled at a man with a mustache and three little minions who kept pushing each other to see me. The beautiful woman, the man with the mustache, and the three annoying minions were my new home. Mi familia.

September 2, 2001. Late at night.

The beautiful woman rocked me in her arms, as she silently cried. "You know baby", she whispered, "mama doesn't seem to have much time left. Mama wishes she could see you and your siblings grow older but baby it seems God has other plans for me". As she softly spoke and carefully moved me with her arms, my eyes were closing. I blinked and caught a glimpse of her slowly wiping the tears from her eyes with her sleeve, "let's keep this a secret between us ok?" As she noticed I was falling asleep, she gently began to put me back on my bed. "Let's not worry your father with my health baby, he's already stressed with work", she said. Then her voice changed, sharply she whispered, "Esmeralda Zenaida Rivera." My eyes shut open, oh hell no I thought, this time I swear I did not do anything wrong if you spank me again I will make sure you never sle- "be strong" she continued "because no matter what Mama will always be by your side." A relieved breath left my lips as I fell back to sleep. That night the last words I heard before I was overcome by darkness were "I love you."

December 12, 2002. 4:31 P.M.

It turned out the dark cave that kept me locked up for months was attacked. The people in white called the attacker "stomach cancer." Apparently, the cancer was stronger than Mama. As Mama got worse, the secret that Mama tried to keep between us, was no longer a secret. Papa found out, but it was too late. At two years old I lost my first home, my mama. I lost the smile that had greeted me every morning, the warm arms that protected me, and the voice that sang me to sleep.

November 3, 2002. Morning.

I now found myself in a new country and in the arms of another woman and man. After Mama passed away, our tía Rosa and tío Diego from Mexico were kind enough to take us in, because it seemed like Papa needed time to get himself together. As the years passed, from oldest to youngest one by one my siblings left me to join Papa. In no time the three annoying minions were no longer around. I was all by myself in Mexico, but as the years passed the memories of Papa, Mama, and my sibling started to fade away. I slowly began to think my tío and tía were my parents and that I was their only child. However, somewhere in the back of my heart, I knew I something was missing.

March 21, 2008. Morning.

I was back to America and in front of me, stood a man. He was wearing a worn out grey coat with a red and brown scarf. His shoes were ripped from the sides and it seemed like he passed his hands through his hair a million times. I knew him. He was first man my eyes came in contact with on my first day on earth. He was the man who lost his wife, his job, and whose blood ran through my veins. Papa was in front of me, with eyes full of sadness and happiness. He then reached out to hold my hand, which I gladly accepted as a smile formed across my face. Papa was finally here, for me and I could not be any happier.

Writing Activity

1. Esmeralda seems to have written a story through a diary. This is an epistolary form, when writing mimics another document to tell a story such as letters, emails, texts, newspaper, diary entries, etc. Try it yourself. Write a story through another form, like a conversation through texts. What does it show you about the way we communicate?

2. There are parts of the story you don't get, Esmeralda even left out years of the story. Why do you think she did this? When time passes in a story, what do you expect to happen? Write a story where you tell a character's story over five years, but only writing about a month for each year.

Rosalinda Avitia Segura

My name is Rosalinda Avitia. I am 18 years old and the youngest in my family. I am currently a freshman in Cal-State Fullerton, studying to be a social worker. Also, I am a proud mother of a baby girl. When you first meet me, I am very shy and seem pretty serious. But once you get to know me, I let my walls fall. I am always there for the people that I love and care for, to the point where I help them more then myself. This is my third year of Barrio Writers, and I have loved every moment of each year. Throughout my years, my friends, family, music and writing have helped me deal with all the problems surrounding me. Everything good or bad in these outcomes has grown me into the person I am today.

Dear Everyone Who Doubts Me And People Like Me,

I am a proud Chicana
Of course I am a Woman
A teen mom
Vaz a escuhar mi voz
In everyone's eyes I am a minority
But I will do better than those who doubt me
Everyone thinks they have the right to comment on my decisions and my life
Pues que creas?
No Puedes
Soy una madre soltera que va atender una Universidad
I will do what you think is not possible
I will do it with pride and a smile on my face to piss you the fuck off
I don't need your negativity
You're probably tired of hearing me rant about this huh?
Guess what?
Me Vale
You need to hear the importance of how I am and people like me are fucking important
Your ignorantasses will be offended and want to build a wall to keep us away
Que creas?
That ain't happening
We will rise and come back stronger
You think we are bad when we are normal
Imagine when you piss us off
Just fucking test us
I suggest you don't though
You will burn from the embarrassment

To The Boy Who Left Us

You say you love me
Sure I believe you
But you don't love me as much as you think
If you did you wouldn't have said the same to the other girls you were sleeping with
If you loved me
You would've heard my screams of pain and the cries of your daughter instead of moans coming from those bitches' mouths
Instead of feeling their hands all over your skin
the warmth and tightness of their body
You would've felt the tears falling from our eyes to your skin
You would've felt our hearts breaking in your chest.
Instead of growing a habit on going to them
You should've grown a connection with your daughter
Because you should've felt your family growing apart from you
Every
Single
Time
you kissed their body
You say you're sorry
But your words no longer have meaning
Instead of letting me in you pushed me out the door and locked me out
I hope you regret the day you let all of this shit happen
Because…
You will regret it the day I call another man my partner
and your daughter calling him daddy.

Update For You

It hurts huh?
Knowing he makes me smile and laugh the way you never did
Knowing that he is the one I go to with everything and anything
That my lust and attention is towards him and only him and forever will be
That I not only give him my body but handed him my heart and soul as well
Knowing that he and only he has made me feel like the most beautiful women he's ever seen

It hurts huh?

Knowing that with just his presence your daughter lights up
Knowing that with just one look
one sound
one word she hears from him she smiles and laughs
That when she wakes up she looks for him and cries for his presence
He taught her how to blow bubbles from her mouth and she does it every single day
Knowing that he knows more of how to calm her down than you
And knowing that he is already the man she calls Apa
He has been more of a man and he is four years younger than you
Knowing…
that you lost us forever
You're just too blind to see it
And too ignorant to accept it

Trash Bags, Roses and…

In Mexico when there's a black draggy trash bag
What's the first thing you think of?
Dead body
Whenever I go visit my family I never see black bags in their draws
Their response?
"Ay no mija no queremos que la gente piense que matamos a personas"
Maybe…
Just maybe..
He should've thrown me in one
But when the trash is already thrown you can never use it again.
That's all he ever did
I thought I was the luckiest person to be with him
Not only be accepted by him but by his friends
They welcomed me into their family of four like I was their missing piece
Made me confident
Made me start believing I have a future
Made me…
Happy
But once he was done he just left me like I was nothing
He decided he didn't need Roses in his garden anymore
He just removed every
Single
One each time he came back
He decided to only keep one and water it whenever he thought it seem fit

Only kept her bloomed when he wanted attention
Until one night…
                    you cut her off from her stem.
That night you just wanted her beauty to yourself
Everything
After ripping off the petals…
            After having his way…
He was probably going to throw me away in that black bag that everyone is afraid off
Maybe…he was going to keep me planted to only water me until he seemed fit again
Sometimes…
Just sometimes…
I wish I were in that stupid black bag
So I won't remember …
        I won't remember why I grew back with so many thorns.

Breathe

I have always lived on the single blue house on Wilshire
It has always been cramped
No space to breathe
        Everything echoing in my ears
Can't fucking think in that house
But I have parents so strict I can barely leave the front porch
Locking myself in my room I start thinking…
                    Dreaming of how I will never let my daughter feel like this
Here let's create the perfect home
I know I will need a huge kitchen
One with six burners on a stove to I can cook every recipe my mother has passed down to me
So I can bake my partner and my daughter the sweets they will crave
A huge refrigerator with everything I need to create my little creations
To the drawers and the covers to store our Mexican vasos, platos, cartones y ollas

Living room can be normal
To the couch
        To the T.V
                    To the family pictures
Maybe that plant that my family always has to have on the center table
The rooms? Normal as well

One for my daughter
Future child
And my future partner and I
I don't need anything fancy in my room
Two attics please
One can be the stereotypical attic with the boxes of old clothes and things we all don't need but are too emotionally attached to throw away
The other one will be the "safe space"
I will have my library of books and comics that I have not separated since third grade
From Spider-Wick to Harry Potter to Vampire Dairies to Spider-Man and The Avengers
My consoles will be there with an old school TV and new one too
I will have from Super Nintendo and Nintendo 64 to PS4 and Nintendo Switch
All the games but mostly from Nintendo because…I grew up with those and I will mostly play Legend of Zelda cause Hello! Best
Game
Ever
Well for me…
I want my backyard to be huge as well
I mean I have to have my lemon tree and orange tree right?
Haha yea,
I want the tree house I never had
I want to have millions of flowers so I can feel the presence of my grandfather
To hear him say
"Ponle agua a las flores mija. Van a crecer hermosas como tu y tu madre"…
I just want space to breathe…
I want to think and think until I have a headache from it
I just don't want to be trapped anymore, breathe.

Apa Chuy

This happens every time I leave
Thinking I left you safe in the home everyone grew up with
I left happy knowing that you were going to stay there until I see you when you come back
Asking you what happened when I was gone and if your brought me my tacos
I would start to take care of you and you would take care of me like we always do
I thought I would hear that raspy voice I can hardly understand but never get

tired of hearing
I thought you would be at my graduation
seeing me walk because I did all
of that for you
I thought you would walk me down the aisle and dance with me on my wedding day
You were suppose to be in the room when my daughter was born
You were suppose to be here for everything…

But right when I heard that last beep
When I saw your eyes close
heard the screams of pain from my aunts and cussing from my uncles
I realized
You weren't going to be present for anything anymore
I realized I didn't leave you safe in your home in Mexicali
You are far away in the heavens to be here…
Even though you aren't here…
You will always be my Apa Chuy

Writing Activity

1. Do you ever feel that people misjudge you because of who you are? What would you like to tell those people about your identity? Write a poem about your pride in your identity. Describe why it is important for others to hear your voice.

2. When words are translated into a different language, sometimes their meaning becomes lost or changed in the translation. Language also carries significant cultural meaning that can be difficult to translate.

Do you speak more than one language? What are some words or phrases that do not translate well into English or have a specific meaning to you? Think about the words from other languages that you have heard growing up. Try to include some of these phrases in your poems or write a poem about a word or phrase from another language.

3. Has anyone ever hurt you in the past? Have you moved on? Are you still dealing with the results of what they did? What would you say to the person that hurt you about how you are living your life now? Write a letter or poem to that person describing how you are moving on with your life.

Moe

Moe is 17 years old and was born on January 24, 2000. She grew up in Santa Ana. She is also the third oldest out of seven children. Even though she was discouraged by others in her family and by her peers, she knew she was worth so much more other than an ordinary half Mexican, half African American girl who couldn't speak or read Spanish. Not saying that as a good or bad thing, but she is serving under her own mission of self-discovery. Moe currently attends Santa Ana Valley High School and has progressed from being the shy girl to so much more. Now being a senior, she has accomplished her fourth year of the Anteater Academy, third year into the Medical Academy, and two years of ASB, Green Club, Health Occupations Students of America, Key Club, and Academic Decathlon. Moe's aspiration in life is to become the first sibling to complete college and apply to medical school in hopes to become a registered nurse while also writing short stories for a youth audience, travel, and inspire others with different ethnic backgrounds.

Who Am I?

I am a woman. Forgive me if it was a bad introduction, I usually write through emotion except this time I'm not emotional. As you can see although my appearance I am what most people would say basic. Just see for yourself what I can tell you is I'm a woman age 17, wearing a lanyard covered in color to unmask the color and beauty to create a vibrant accessory not just because it is a lanyard. This lanyard addresses who I am. Who Am I? Unfortunately, I cannot describe through every detail because instead of describing who I am one thing I can say is that I am a woman. However, it's not the only thing I know. Regardless of my age I know that I AM CREATIVE, I AM VIBRANT, and I AM THOUGHTFUL. I also like my mistakes and I like the pace of my mistakes, because mistakes are not only something I can learn it is something I can LAUGH and CRY. Ironically, I'm apologetic…that's what my mistakes consists of me doing. I say sorry too much. I think too much. Most importantly I cry too much because I constantly crave to learn. So regardless of what you know, this is who I am… I am someone who is not as open as these words appear to you and that's okay.

What have I lost? What have I gained?

What I have lost is the voice inside to divide, to conquer the obstacles which in the past made me who I am today. To elaborate I've lost the drive to be successful I am a cup that is half empty and hides in the dark abyss waiting, wanting to be in the sunlight to again be filled with the knowledge and achievement to succeed. What I have gained is the silence that prevents me to speak my mind, to speak my emotion, to speak of solutions yet instead I have gained illusions. Illusions that are against the occurring reality of what is happening around me. This prevents me to speak my voice and find a solution for my mother of 7 children including myself to leave my father without struggling in what will lead to her being homeless and us being in the foster system. The silence has driven me to starve both physically and mentally into me focusing a bottomless depth of failures rather than victories. I am a car radio with no sound thus creates an awkward silence to others around my surroundings. However, without creating the empty voice I have gained the wiliness of self-discovery, to find my strength/weakness that describes me who I want to be. I've gained the lyrics to what is an unfinished song which has a purpose is to be heard and give hope to others who have also lost the voice… the sound. Therefore, this discussion of what I've lost and gained is bittersweet yet it is the question that is difficult to answer. Do I have enough of what I can deliver to myself and others?

Peer-Pressure

You're different with others but you're a pain with me.
Every time I say no, you encourage me to say YES.
You give me illusions that only give me false hope of how things will be when I do it, if I do it.
However, I don't hate you.
You helped me meet new people, try new opportunities.
Yet all you can say is "Everyone is doing it".
Yet the funny thing is the memories I think of when we were together…
There were horrible.
You're horrible.
You've pushed me down, chewed me up, and spit me back out when it's over.
You make me do things I don't want to do.
For Christ Sake I lost my virginity in a parking lot… cause of you.
You hurt me.
Humiliate me.
Make me crave for attention yet you take all the fame.
"Everyone's doing it so why shouldn't I?"
You make me think that everyone I know is popping pills.
Getting high yet on the side, you come along and I feel trapped.
Because out of everyone I gave most of my power, to you.
All I can say now is "God, please forgive me, and give me the strength to accept the things I cannot change."

Just know if I could change anything in this world…
I would change your attitude.
Matter of fact, upgrade.
Instead of encouraging me to do my best, I end up doing the worst because what I do is ask for the attention and gain the approval of irrelevant people.
You're irrelevant.
But that's not what I came to tell you.
I wanted to say Thank you and provide you with a little bit of advice.
Don't get bitter, get better.

Writing Activity

1. Moe titles her stories with questions. This can be an effective technique as questions tend to need answers. Try it yourself. Ask yourself a question and then write a response. Let that response be a story or poem.

2. There are many things that affect us as people and not for the better. Moe's poem "Peer-Pressure" takes a bad influence in her life and explores it. What influences you in a negative way? Write a poem with that bad influence as the title, and explore it.

Alma Peguero

Alma Peguero was born on March 27, 2000. She is 17 years old. Some of her bad habits are: procrastinating on school work due to her immense love of literature, eating a slice of vegan carrot cake before hitting the gym, and allowing stress to overflow making her forget that Sunday is laundry day.

In an attempt to get out of her comfort zone, Alma has shared her writing every year of high school and has found overpowering joy in doing so. She aspires to become a successful book critic and writer.

Aconitum

There's a soreness in my knuckles when I bend my fingers,
Spots of auburn blanketing the slopes

I know I bruised your pretty little face
I can see the heat radiating from your cheeks
in shame as the people around note the blend
of red and blue behind those cheap sunglasses you bought.
Your blush turns crimson from the rays of the sun in the
summer afternoon, sweat dripping from the crease of your
forehead, down your unblemished neck to the collar of
your long-sleeved shirt.

I won't apologize to you because there is no
reason to apologize when I know you'll take my silence as a cue
to drop to your knees in our living room,
your apology written by the swirl of your tongue
and by the frantic dance of your head.

Your lips opening wide enough for me,
leaving trails of spit running down your chin, and
you hum around me, hoping that it'll make me feel good.
But you look so pathetic looking up at me with those hopeful eyes.

When I'm done, push you to the side
without asking if you're okay
because I know you want me to hold you.
I know you'll bare your neck to me,
expecting brushes of my lips on your shoulders
when you don't deserve that.
If I were to kiss you there

it wouldn't be with my lips or tongue,
it would be my teeth trying to break your skin.
And you'll cry, not because you feel good
but because I rejected every bit of you.

I'm not with you for the sex.
You just provide me that.
And I take it because you spread your legs
like an opportunity.

You'd crawl through burning sand just so that
I provide you with what you think must be
love.

To you I am this majestic man who has what he wants.
You don't know that I'd burn my tongue
than ever tell you that I love you
even if meant that you'd leave.

I refuse to say those three empty
words through my clenched teeth.
And you refuse to open your
God damn eyes and
realize how toxic we are.

If it weren't for you, I would be as alone
as you are in my presence,
you don't even realize how alone you are.

But,

Everything about us works, because I know
I have you wrapped around my little finger.

Estime de Soi

Another night in your room, you're lying on the blue blankets of your bed. Red rosy cheeks pressed against your pillow, it becomes hard to suppress the grin that threatens to spill over your physiognomy. He is, as John Albee once wrote, "Beautiful as a remembered single line of perfect poetry." You think about him all the time, with the one sentence repeating over and over again, "I like him so much."

You then make your way to the bathroom with the thought of wanting to look pretty the next day, with the shirt you bought from the thrift store and the necklace that holds a stone that represents luck which is cliché but you hold onto the hope that it grants you just that. The lift of your cheeks leaves your face muscles sore, but that smile is gone when you find yourself in front of the mirror. Bare, naked, unclothed, undressed. Those words make your breath hitch because you hate the way you look so vulnerable, and you just know everyone is dreading the day they have to see you anything close to naked.

The flush of your cheeks is gone, substituted by the chilling air of your home and goosebumps rising from your skin. It's the voice of your father warning you that he also needs to shower that makes you turn the knobs in the bathtub to a pleasing temperature, and you're suddenly wishing people found you as pleasing as the lukewarm water descending upon the vast curves of skin.

When you're done, your soaked body stands in front of the mirror again, and you are thankful for the fogged mirror that blurs your image and thankful for that God awful eyesight that could kill you if it weren't for the invention of spectacles.

You go to bed wondering how these thoughts have taken over your mind the whole night when you were only thinking about how good he looked with that freckle on his hand. Self-hatred permits these pessimistic thoughts to intoxicate your head right before you close your eyes for the long-anticipated sleep.

At school, you don't say anything. There are people who tell you to be outgoing and social but the moment you open your simpleminded mouth, they are baffled. Your voice is a little too loud, your laugh is a little too boisterous. Your laugh is uncontrolled, breathless, some will call it contagious others will find themselves in the throbbing state of mind called annoyance. That quiets you.

But people hate that you're quiet, you look a little too sad, you look a little too unapproachable. The frown looks revolting on you but you don't have the energy to curl the corner of your lips in the slightest.

You are dull.

You are repulsive.

You are infuriating.

But then there are those who are the epitome of celestial beings who like you and genuinely appreciate you.

To them you are:

Beautiful.

Intelligent.

Ethereal.

To them you are enough.

Fluent

Don't laugh at me with your mouth full
Your laugh overly exaggerated, completely cynical.
You look disgusting, your laugh stretching your tongue out
Pushing the breadcrumbs past your lips.

Don't laugh at me for attempting to speak our
Native language when English has clearly dominated
My vocabulary.

Don't get bothered with me when
I ask for the house keys in English when
You're the reason I can't speak in
Spanish comfortably.

Don't expect me to confide in you on
How I've sunk down so low
And have joined a Spanish 1 class.
You'd be ashamed for me
While I'm trying to better myself.

Once I can speak in rapid Spanish,
Fluently,
No hesitation,
Don't expect me to read you
Shakespeare in Spanish.

You are simply not worth it.

Writing Activity

1. Aconitum is a type of flower. Why do you think Alma titled a poem after a flower, when the poem isn't necessarily about flowers? Write a poem where you title it after something, but don't talk about the item in the poem. What meaning does it give to the item?

2. Alma wrote a piece in 2nd person point of view. 2nd person is when the writing is addressed to 'you' rather in 1st person (I, me, us, we) or 3rd person (he, she, they, them). Write a story where you use 'you' to refer to the character. What does that do to the reader?

Shyla Driver

Shyla Driver was born and raised in Nacogdoches, Texas, where she attends Nacogdoches High School as a junior and Stephen F. Austin as a freshman. She plays tenor saxophone in her school marching band and is a member of theatre. She hopes to become a speech language pathologist or work in video game music development.

An Open Letter to Education

Dear Education,

As you read (or listen to) this letter, I want you to appreciate the grammar, format, and overall dedication put into this letter, especially because you have taught me none of those things.

I should start off with paragraphs. I've been writing stories since the first grade and essays since the fourth grade, but I never understood the concept of a paragraph. In fact, in grade four, my teacher, the woman who was supposed to teach me how to write an essay, wrote essays for us at the beginning of the year, and had us memorize them by our TAKS test in March.

However, I finally understood what a paragraph was at age 12. I had learned from fanfiction.net where I had spent hours upon hours reading stories, until it finally clicked: a paragraph is a series of related complete thoughts. When we did have to write paragraphs, they would always say, "Oh, just write 3-5 sentences." That's not a paragraph! That's 3-5 sentences.

Let's move onto something a little simpler, shall we: the alphabet. I'd really love to start with phonics, but you can no longer teach phonics past Pre-K – a grade which children aren't even required to attend. Still on the subject of the alphabet, I was once working on a homework sheet with a boy in my Spanish I class. I don't exactly remember the grammatical concept but it was important to understand the difference between vowels and consonants. The boy I was working with, a fellow sophomore, didn't know what a vowel was.

And Education, I see you over there with your smug face and crossed arms. You say, "You're just complaining about English, not education." Well, Education, that's because I'm getting plenty of extra instruction.

I mean, I can't do taxes but I can sure as heck find you the inverse of a matrix. I can't sew but I know the parts of a cell. About half of my female friends think they urinate from their vagina, but what would any of them do if they couldn't use the Pythagorean theorem to solve the distance of a lake.

Secretary DeVos – I mean, Education – please don't prepare me for a world that doesn't exist. A world where I solve for exponential decay and write essays for the negative effects of the Columbian Exchange. Teach me how to defend myself. Teach me how to hold a job.

Education, I've been here 11 years. Can't you teach me something?

A Modern Fairy Tale That Has Not Received a Title

For what must've been the thousandth time, obsidian ink hit the ivory canvas. It seemed every time she put her paint to the board, she'd do something wrong, but now, it seemed like she was finally getting the hang--

"MOTHER--" Nature was being more than fickle today. The thousandth attempt she made went well for about forty seconds until a leaf hit her canvas and smeared the black ink. She muttered obscenities under her breath as she tore yet another off the set of white papers. The purchase of paper she made yesterday had now only left seven, causing her to groan.

"'Move to Osaka,' they said. 'They have beautiful autumns,' they said." Artemis reached for her brush once more, but before she could get to it, she heard her phone ringing.

She was on the line for at least two minutes but all she heard was stuttering, stammering, and crying. She had only gathered the words, "Dump," "Cheat," and, "Pick me up." With a frustrated sigh, she snatched up her easel, and headed inside to go save her useless roommate.

She walked back inside, gray shoes hitting white tile, gray feet hitting black carpet. She sat down her easel when all of a sudden she heard...laughing?

But that couldn't be. The only ones who had a key to her house were her roommate and herself. Artemis decided to walk against the wall, as to not be seen.

She peered around the corner to see a boy. On the couch. Watching TV. There were at least seven Coca-Cola cans scattered around him and another one in his hand. The couch was still black, the can of coke still had its same gray luster, but the boy... The boy wore a bright orange shirt and trash green denim pants. His skin was the color of caramel and his hair was the color of ground coffee beans. This boy was... mortified, actually.

When he saw her he froze for a moment. After a few seconds he shot up from the couch and out the door. Artemis had a lot of questions at the moment, but the biggest was, why the boy left behind a trail of colorful sparkles. And how could she see them?

Beside where had sat there was a book of Japanese folklore. It was open to a page and there was writing on a drawing of one of the demons that read, "I look nothing like that." She looked at the name of the demon in the picture.

"Nu...ra...ri – hyon." Between the third and fourth syllable, the book had disappeared. The only thing left in her hands were the same colorful sparkles the boy had left behind. But color was not something she was supposed to see.

And she supposed, neither was that boy.

Unbridled #2

I don't feel American.
I never have.
It didn't occur to me until the one time I did.

The only time I ever felt American
Was in another country
Why do I have to leave to feel like a part of my own home?

Writing Activity

1. In "An Open Letter," the speaker demands that education teach her "how to defend herself" and "how to hold a job." Do you feel the same way about your education system? What actions can you take to teach yourself when a system has "failed you"?

2. In "A Modern Fairy Tale That has not Received a Title," what do you think the significance of Artemis seeing everything except Nurarihyon in monochrome? Have you ever seen things in a way that others have not? What was that like? Try doing some free writing about the experience and see where it takes you.

Yasmeen Davila

Yasmeen Davila, 21, is from Pasadena TX. A first generation xicana, she studies history and economics at the University of Texas at Austin. A member of Native American and Indigenous Collective, Native American and Indigenous Peoples, International Indigenous Youth Council, and University Leadership Initiative she dedicates her activism around exposing colonial structures of communal division.

sin voz

Sucked to the past, 14 years from today. I am sitting at my assigned seat busy minding my own, laughing at inappropriate times. I am in 3rd grade.

A bright day outside. Our beans in plastic bags hanging from the window covering its brightness.

My teacher Ms. Silvia is rushing towards the furthest part of the classroom where the carpet and miniature library lay. The only place I knew of relaxation in the classroom. But this seemed like an odd occasion. As we settled on the carpet she rambled about a paper written by someone in the class.

No. No, she wasn't complimenting the student.

"This is by far one of the worst papers I have read."

Mind you that she has been teaching for over 12 years.

That carpet. That big block-like, colorful, numbered, alphabetized. My eyes wandered over its playfulness. My fingers tapping, flickering, running, and outlining that carpet replicated in every elementary school as I came to find out.

I snapped back out of my wandering nervous thoughts. I was anxious at the thought that the paper in her hands she so eloquently began to read to the class was mine.

I listened. I looked around at the faces that surrounded me.

"I said that… I think I said that… did I say that?" I questioned myself wanting with every inch of my existence for it to be a classmates' paper.

"I remember writing that," my final thought.

The realization slowly embraced my body. Noticing the warmth of my body, I felt red. Flushed.

"Yasmeen Davila" she announced. She stood looking over all of us until her eyes landed on mine. To this day I wonder what she saw. Does she remember my facial expression? How did she feel at the moment? A thrill?

I don't remember her face. I looked through her. I saw nothing but my inner thoughts.

Everyone looked at me sorrowfully or so I think this is part of the memory. I didn't hide. I was sitting next to Ms. Silvia. I could only accept the waves of emotions this event rippled through my being for years to come.

Not too long had passed before there was a call to the class asking for Mels, Pearls, Liz and I to go to another class.

Did I forget to mention I was in G.T.? A program I had no idea how I had gotten into, but I didn't ask questions then. My parents were happy when they were told I was gifted and talented. I went with it.

Ms. Silvia had gotten her assistant/intern to accompany us to the G.T. class and reclaim me for my embarrassing writing. [She was not willing to leave a child behind.]

I walked into the portable classroom having had a short walk in the heavy heated air before arriving. I walked in the room distracted, nervous, embarrassed, sad. My voice? Sin voz.

I knew two languages but there were no words in my mouth.

There are bad teachers.

Close to horrible teachers.

But there are also inspiring and empowering ones.

Ms. Sarabia, my G.T. teacher, was one of them. She almost laughed at the request of my removal from the program she supervised. "I will work with her on her writing."

Simple. Clear. Direct.

Her words did not fill the room, her voice did not rise, her posture polished her response.

Spit back out to the present. It has been 14 years since the incident. I have accumulated more traumatizing experiences since then, but those I will save for another story.

I survived through advanced placement courses. I learned to love reading and I have begun writing for leisure.

I have held on to these memories because they play with my heart. They bring back emotions I wish to never feel again.

I found myself voiceless. I had an illusion of what education was and how I was supposed to work through the system. All of which equated to my being without a say on what happened to me.

I keep these memories close to me now because they have held me and have poked me in discomfort only to bring about the way I express myself.

I have regained the voice I longed for by using everything in my physical being and these memories that have followed me today. I speak volumes without using a word.

I have cut my hair to the point where a joke about my armpit hair being longer than the hair on my head would not be too farfetched.

I reprimand myself for focusing on my appearance. But the attention I receive because of the sexualization of my body makes me focus on it even more.

My armpit hair stands as if a balloon had been rubbed on it, static-y.

I refresh my sweaty pits in the air-conditioned public bus. The gleeful eyes fueled by my sexualization go soft and regrettably look outside the window. I am less annoyed and always satisfied at men's response to my body hair. I continue to refresh myself from the Texas heat inside the black smoke spitting bus.

I run in a family with a beautiful sense of humor.

I use my body, my hair, my appearance to speak for me. I giggle in front of the mirror looking at my arm pit hair, bothering everyone all the while it's minding its own. I do not speak much even with friends because I feel no need to. I only speak when I am moved, when I have something that needs to be said. Soft and strong.

I stand my ground by my simple face expression, my posture, my appearance, and honesty. "Firme," I am firm.

Writing Activity

1. Write about a time in which you were silenced by an adult or someone who had power over you.

2. Yasmeen re-creates a memory that incorporates descriptive details using the five senses. Take the piece you wrote for Writing Activity 1 and revise it by incorporating descriptive details that show the moment like you are watching a scene in a movie.

3. Although we are faced with traumatic experiences, we often find ways to empower ourselves later and regain our voice. Consider how Yasmeen does this at the end of her piece by repeating affirming "I" statements. Write your own addition to your piece or begin an "I am" poem that describes who you are.

Keona D. Redmon

Keona is a young artist and writer born in Austin, Texas. She hopes to continue her work in art after college and possibly make it a career.

They Say

They say I am bottled up
I ask "when will the bottle open?"

They say I'm quiet
I say "I sometimes need expert advice"

They say I am inexperienced
I say "I'm still learning to fly"

They say I can be clumsy
I tell them "I just have skills that nobody wants"

They say I'm random
I say "I prefer to call it a unique personality"

They say I'm strange
I tell them I see things differently

They say I look weird
I say "I'm glad I don't look like anyone else"

They say I lack a sense of humor
I tell them they just don't understand

They say I always leave a mess
I say "It's to remember me by"

The Flower

It's a leaf in the ground.
Over time it splits in two, and out comes a seed
The leaves curl,
the flower sprouts,
After weeks the leaves are dead.
The seedling is big and still growing
and sprouting more seeds
to fly through the wind
One by one they leave,
To bring beauty to other places
Now you just see the bare and hollow shell
More seeds grow in and soon attract pests and other animals
You are slowly picked apart and eaten.
You have almost reached your limit and are falling apart
the poor little flower truly dead at heart.
Now you are covered by snow,
your beauty can not be seen
Just like that you're gone,
hoped to come again next spring.

Writing Activity

1. Keona takes criticisms of the speaker's 'faults' and turns them into positives. For example, rather than thinking of someone as quiet, maybe they don't need the words of people in that room. This is a form of empathy. Rather than only believing one way about someone or yourself, try to see that person from another angle. Write a poem where you take a criticism of something or someone and consider their point of view. Is it a flaw in their character? Or is it a flaw of society?

2. What a writer chooses to write about reveals a little something about them and/or the speaker. In 'The Flower,' the speaker focuses on the growth of a flower. What do we see and/or learn about the flower and the speaker? Write a poem about an aspect of nature and see what you focus on.

CPSIA information can be obtained
at www.ICGtesting.com
Printed in the USA
BVHW03s1659030818
523125BV00003B/8/P

9 781622 882151